Our love —

To Mary and Bill

Christmas, 1955

Ellie and Anna

HILAIRE BELLOC

HILAIRE BELLOC

A Memoir

by J. B. MORTON

SHEED & WARD • NEW YORK

Dedicated to
the Family of Hilaire Belloc
and to All His Friends

CONTENTS

PREFACE

THERE IS NO ART BY WHICH A DEAD MAN MAY BE SO PRE-
sented to the living that those who knew him will seem to
have seen him once more as he was, and those who did not
know him will receive the plenary effect of his personality.
A portrait or a bust may give to posterity his image, may
even persuade us that the skill of artist or sculptor has presented for the living not only his likeness, but even the elements of his character. One who was his friend may recognize the qualities which the skill of the interpreter has
transferred to canvas or to clay. One who never saw him
may say, standing before the bust or the portrait, "Evidently he was a man of this kind or that." Perhaps a writer
will describe him so persuasively, and in detail so vivid,
that the sleeping memories of his friends are awakened as
though by magic, and his very gestures and movements
return to them for a moment. But nothing, nothing can
bring back the whole man, the full man, the living man.
The bust is dead matter, the portrait will not breathe, the
words are only words. We cannot hear the tones of a voice
stilled for ever, nor see the animation of the features, the
swift changes of expression in the eyes, the play of emotion over the face. Yet always, if there is to be a memorial
to the dead, something must be attempted.

In this brief memoir will be found some account of a
great man who was also the greatest writer of his day. I
was honoured with his friendship for a period of thirty

years. Of his life before I knew him I have written little,
since that is a task for his biographers. Such references as
I have made to the years preceding 1922 were necessary
to the telling of my story, and my information on those
earlier years is drawn from his writings, from the autobiography of his sister, Mrs. Belloc Lowndes, and from his
conversations with me. For the account of the accident
upon which his death followed so quickly, and for certain
other facts, I am indebted to his daughter, Mrs. Reginald
Jebb; and to Mrs. Peter Belloc I express my gratitude for
permission to read her father-in-law's letters to Peter Belloc and to herself, two of which she has allowed me to
print.

J. B. MORTON

1

PORTRAIT OF HILAIRE BELLOC

THE VILLAGE OF LA CELLE-SAINT-CLOUD STANDS ON THE wooded heights above the left bank of the Seine, in a part of the Ile-de-France which many French artists have preserved for us in their paintings. It is a countryside too near Paris to have remained what it was before the coming of the motor-car, but something of its enchantment may still be found today. There is a quality in the air and in the colours of the landscape which induces a mood of reverie. At dawn and at dusk come those strange glints of far-away light which enchanted Watteau, and the mist, so tenuous that it seems an illusion, which is delicate as a breath in Corot's pictures of the quiet lake-waters of Ville-d'Avray. It is also a countryside rich in historical memories of the French Monarchy and of Napoleon. All about La Celle are the great woods where the French kings hunted. St. Germain is its neighbour; and St. Cloud, where the stroke of Brumaire so nearly failed; all that remains of the splen-

1

dour of Marly; and Louveciennes, where Mme. du Barry
had her house. To Louveciennes, along the old road from
Versailles painted by Sisley and Manet, André Chénier
would come to meet "Fanny" (Mme. Lecoulteux). At Ville
d'Avray is Corot's lake, and in the woods of Meudon
Manon Roland walked. Below La Celle is Malmaison,
where the Empress Josephine died, and where Napoleon,
listening to the bells of Rueil, recalled his youth. A mile or
so from Rueil St. Geneviève was born in the hamlet of
Nanterre, and across the river is Chatou. Here, in 1815,
Bulow, ordered by Blücher to seize the Emperor at Malmaison, found the bridge destroyed, and heard that Napoleon had started on the journey to Rochefort.

Between Sèvres and Bougival the Seine makes one of its
horseshoe loops. From Bougival, which faces Croissy, the
home of Paul Déroulède and his family across the river, a
road goes up to La Celle-Saint-Cloud. On this road, in a
house outside the village, now No. 8 Avenue Camille Nor-
mand, Hilaire Belloc was born on July 27th, 1870.

All day the woods had been still in the heavy air of high
summer, but shortly before his birth a violent thunder-
storm broke. It was long remembered and talked of, and
when the child who was born on that day was in a temper,
his mother would call him "Old Thunder." But, at his birth
there was another kind of thunder in the air. From Belfort
to Strasbourg the ill-organized and imperfectly equipped
French armies were coming into position along the old
frontier of invasion, and eastward, on the roads and railways, moved the artillery and the supply-trains; so that
one might say that Hilaire Belloc was born to the sound of
the rumble of guns. During the first week of his life, the
failure of the French Intelligence and the feebleness of
administration and command allowed the Prussian General Staff to complete their preparations for the invasion
of France. On August 4th the German Third Army crossed

the frontier, and two days later was fought the battle of Woerth. There followed the French retreat through the defiles of the Vosges. The child was two weeks old when those in the house at La Celle-Saint-Cloud heard the heavy guns going by to Mont Valérien. The tragedy of Sedan and the march on Paris followed. The Republic was proclaimed, and it was only in September that Hilaire and his sister Marie were taken to England by their parents. The train in which they left Paris was the last to run before the siege began.

❖   ❖   ❖   ❖   ❖

Three strains of blood were mingled in Hilaire Belloc: English, French and Irish. His mother, Elizabeth Parkes, was the daughter of Joseph Parkes, who played a prominent part at the time of the Reform Bill, and has a statue in Birmingham today. Her great-grandfather was Joseph Priestley the scientist. The family was of strong Unitarian stock, but in 1864 Elizabeth Parkes was received into the Catholic Church. She had been active in the campaign for Women's Rights, and had known well most of the great Victorians. She married, in 1867, Louis, the son of the celebrated painter Hilaire Belloc and of Louise Swanton Belloc, a well-known writer and a woman of great beauty and charm. This lady was the daughter of Colonel Swanton, the last Colonel of the Berwick Brigade, who served under Napoleon; and the niece of Baron Chasseriau, who was killed in that great cavalry charge at Waterloo, described by Wellington as the finest feat of arms he had ever seen. Seven of the Baron's brothers fought in Napoleon's armies. It was from the Swantons that the Irish strain came into the Belloc blood. Mrs. Belloc Lowndes has provided, in her volumes of autobiography, a detailed account of her ancestry, and has described the background of the family life at La Celle-Saint-Cloud, and the early years of herself and her brother. The circumstances of Hilaire Belloc's boyhood, with one home in England and another in France, and his mixed blood, had their effect on his ideas, and explain, to some extent, his diversity, and the apparent contradictions in his character. The mixture of Victorian England and Republican France was clearly visible in him.

His wit was French, but his humour English. He was profoundly moved by the beauty of English landscape, but preferred the French way of living. His military temper, his love of justice rather than order, the logical processes of his thought were French. At sea he was English, but Irish in that recurring dream of a landfall which is not of this world. Some have called him, for his hearty pugnacity, a figure as English as Cobbett. Others have emphasized his many un-English qualities. In appearance he seemed to be an Englishman dressed as a Frenchman.

I suppose that if you asked a hundred people who knew him, what struck them most about him they would answer: "His physical and intellectual vitality." In the earliest of his portraits of him, James Gunn has captured that vitality. Belloc is sitting back in a chair, but the grip of the right hand on the arm of the chair suggests that he will be on his feet in a minute. Anyone who knew him says, on looking at this portrait, "How often I have seen him in exactly that attitude." The left hand rests on his left knee, with the little finger bent back (it was injured by a boathook in his youth). The strong face is stamped with intelligence. Though he is at rest, his whole attitude is combative. The square shoulders and the heavy body produce an impression of energy and power which the jaw and the set of the lips confirm.

Belloc's vitality would have been remarkable if it had been confined to the production of more than one hundred and fifty works over a period of forty-six years. But those years were also filled with travel, with sailing, and with the enjoyment of life among friends. He was, as every-body knows, a tremendous talker, interested in an unusual variety of subjects and curious about every aspect of human affairs. An old friend of the family who saw him when, in early youth, he was walking across America[1] and paying his way by making and selling sepia sketches, described the violent energy of his talk as a most remarkable experience. That energy was expressed, not by copious gesture, but by the vigour of his voice, by his choice of language, and by the force of what is called personality. What always struck me was his exceptionally wide range of knowledge, the rapidity of his speech, and his habit of changing, in a flash, the plane of his talk. He would interpolate a jest into a serious monologue, or pierce the comedy of a description with a shaft of poetry. He never talked for effect or for the sake of talking, never feigned emotion, used no trick of insincerity to score a point. He indulged little in epigram, but when he did make an epigram, it was an epigram, not simply a clever saying. It was the fruit of wisdom, and experience of men and things. His orderly mind delighted in precise definition, and he was always irritated by what he called "muddled thinking." I have said that he used gesture sparingly; being, in that, English, not French. But one French gesture he had. He would lay his index finger to his nose occasionally, or wag it to and fro when he disagreed with you. In the course of a discussion he would marshal his arguments by holding up a finger for "Point one"; then two, then three fingers, and so on. In conversation as an exchange of triv-

[1] In 1889 he had met, in his mother's house in London, the girl with whom he fell in love at first sight, Elodie Hogan. In 1890 he went to America by steerage, to persuade her to marry him. They were engaged for seven years, and it was only after Belloc had done his military service in France and finished his brilliant career at Oxford that they were married, in 1896. Her Irish grandparents had emigrated, during the Famine, to California.

ialities he was not interested, and it was a common experience among his friends to abandon what they were saying when he entered a room, as he was almost sure to make some startling remark, and then to follow it up. You could often guess what subject his next book would be about, because he would be full of it. His manner was emphatic, and like all abundant talkers, he used exaggeration. He once wrote: "Watch your contemporaries, and you will notice that a man who talks a great deal, talks a great deal of nonsense, and that a man who talks very little, hardly ever talks sense." Sometimes he contradicted himself, and sometimes he talked nonsense, but as he said, when writing of Napoleon's talk: "When you read his sayings—chance, irritable, merry, determined—distinguish between the categories: for he was a man who talked and talked and talked all the time, having—to put it without exaggeration—a creative brain." And he marvelled that anyone should take seriously chance sayings, "or make of exact verbal consistency a necessity for their own self-respect."[1] Things thrown off, exclamations, outbursts, must never be treated as serious judgments.

This vitality of his, then, is obvious to the readers of his books and to those who heard him talk. His restlessness was also a part of it. He could never be idle, and liked to have his whole day planned, hour by hour. Vitality was also apparent in his walk; rapid, short steps, like a Chasseur Alpin on the march, except that he barely raised his feet from the ground. It was apparent, again, in his capacity for doing a number of things simultaneously—for instance, he could carry on a discussion while correcting proofs and ordering a meal. Yet again, it was apparent in his mobile features, in the quick movement of his head, in his swift and decisive way of beginning or breaking off a

[1] Preface to *The St. Helena Journal of General Baron Gourgand.* (The Bodley Head: 1932.)

conversation, in his hearty likes and dislikes, in his loud happiness and his ferocious angers.

Next to vitality, what always struck me in him was courtesy. To many who never knew him this will seem an eccentric thing to say. He was regarded, and rightly, as a pugnacious man, a hardened controversialist, and had, in some quarters, a reputation for bluntness or even down-right rudeness. Like any hot-blooded man who is in the midst of debates which he takes seriously, Belloc could be ruthlessly outspoken when he wanted to. But he was essentially a courteous man. His manners were old-fash-ioned—and all the better for that. To the end of his life he bowed over your hand, and had always ready one of those conventional phrases of politeness which sound so odd to-day. If you offered to do him the smallest service, he al-ways said, not "Thanks," but "This is really very kind of you." As for doing anyone else a service, no trouble was too much for him. Many are the friends who, having con-sulted him on an itinerary abroad, have received detailed advice on where to stay, what to see, and even what to eat and drink. If you sent him a book written by yourself, he, who read little outside old favourites and books connected with his work, would write a long letter back, flattering by its very length. He, who could denounce so heartily and to such purpose, loved to praise, and what he did for *The Diary of a Nobody*, for Mr. P. G. Wodehouse, and for Ernest Bramah, is common knowledge. I remember once telling him how much I had enjoyed a book. He said: "Write and tell him so. One ought always to do that when one likes people's books. It bucks them up." He himself received praise with a kind of innocent pleasure, and humbly.

In social matters he was more than polite; he was unfail-ingly considerate, for instance, in the difficult task (espe-cially in London nowadays) of punctuality. If he was likely to arrive late, by however small a margin, he telephoned to his host or hostess to tell them that he was detained. Often he telephoned if he thought he was likely to arrive before the time of the engagement. He was always sending telegrams, either to confirm an engagement made in a letter, or some appointment about which he had been doubtful. I cannot recall an occasion when he failed to give ample warning of a breakdown of his plans. If he was not sure of reaching you with a letter or a telegram, or could not telephone, he sent a duplicate letter to an alternative address. I have many such messages sent to me in the country and in London, and asking for confirmation. When he gave any trouble by his fussiness over food, he was always apologetic, nor ever took for granted the desire to please him and make him comfortable. Being so punctilious himself, he expected a similar thoughtfulness in return, and one of the things he could not tolerate was the unexpected arrival of anybody at King's Land, his home in Sussex, without previous arrangement. He did not take easily to strangers, and no man could put the presumptuous in their place with a more frigid politeness. It is a common thing for someone in a bar to approach a well-known writer, with some such opening as, "You won't remember me. We met at ———." When that occurred Belloc was guarded, but never offensive. If the interloper was obviously an impostor, and would not be dismissed, he was given to understand that he was making a nuisance of himself—which is the only way to deal with such an affair. There is a story that Belloc was accosted after a lecture by a man who said, "You don't remember me," and that Belloc replied, "Oh, yes, I do," and walked away. I can conceive such a thing happening, if the man was recognized as a professional pesterer of the famous. Otherwise, I think it an unlikely tale.

A celebrity has always to be prepared to be misrepresented and misquoted, and Belloc had his share of this. Somebody starts an anecdote on its travels, it is repeated, finds its way into print, and the mischief is done. No amount of subsequent contradiction can kill the story. It is firmly entrenched. Many times I have heard people quote "How odd of God to choose the Jews," and attribute it to Belloc. Once this happened in his presence, and he said, "That's not the way I write." But people continue to attribute it to him, probably because of the false idea that he was what is called "anti-Semitic." He liked or disliked a Jew as he liked or disliked any other man, and he wrote a book called *The Jews*, which those who called him an "anti-Semite" should have taken the trouble to read.

Belloc had the virtue of humility. He had pride, but no vanity. It was his conviction that it is ridiculous to be conceited about a good poem or a majestic piece of prose, because the writer is only the tool used to produce a certain effect. Inspiration comes to him from outside himself, not from within. He was grateful for praise, but when it was fulsome, he treated it as a joke, and he liked to read out, with gusts of laughter, extravagant compliments paid to him by critics. On the many occasions when I heard a friend compliment him on a piece of work, he said, "That's very kind of you," and was obviously uncomfortable if the compliment went on too long. "Hero-worship is intolerable," he used to say. This attitude was due partly to his highly developed sense of humour, which is only sense of proportion, and keeps one sane and balanced. But it was due more to humility, to the conviction, which I have mentioned, that a man is a fool to give himself airs, and to take all the credit for what he has written.

He loved to boast, but the boasting was of that outrageous kind which nobody takes seriously. He and Philip Kershaw used to have boasting contests when they were walking or sailing together, and his son Peter inherited the taste. It is a healthy pastime, and a boast can be a weapon, as in the case of that Gascon who fought under Napoleon. A slimy little man said to him: "Life must be very hard and primitive in your stormy mountains. How on earth do you keep warm in the winter?" And the Gascon answered: "Oh, we burn the batons of some of the Marshals in our family." The boasting was part of his high spirits and his sense of humour, and anyone who, after meeting him in his swashbuckling mood, had been told that he was a humble man, would have had to understand what Catholics mean by humility, to make sense of such a remark. He was conspicuous in any company, not because he pushed himself forward, or made a claim to distinction, but because he was a man different from those around him; to put it precisely—a great man. His appearance was striking—the black clothes, the cloak, the French gunner's halfboots, the stick-up stiff collar of a past age, the formal, almost ceremonial manners. But far more striking was the man himself. At the end of his life his humility helped him to endure with resignation long years of inactivity, and the deprivations which his failing strength made necessary. For all the times I heard him complain of the disappointments of his life, I never once heard him even hint that he had deserved something better. That is humility.

His sense of humour was unfailing. It was not merely the ability to make a joke or to appreciate somebody else's joke. It was a sane and healthy way of looking at life, so that he never attached undue importance to what is relatively unimportant. His sense of humour was not dependent on a mood. It was not a matter of being in good spirits. It was there, and active, all the time, playing like a fountain. His enjoyment of the comedy of human existence prevented him from becoming too embittered, and kept him essentially simple. As words are used today, he would be called sophisticated, and a compliment would be intended. He knew the world's usage and the motives of men. But in the older and true meaning of the word, he was not sophisticated: that is, his knowledge and wide experience had not warped or adulterated his nature. He knew, as any intelligent man knows, that what we are all seeking is not to be found in the brief years on earth. That habit of complaining, and of saying that life was a digusting thing, was like the vigorous protests of a sailor in a storm or a soldier under shell-fire. It helped him to go on with what he had to do. It was when he was in his prime that he protested most loudly. At the end of his life, when he had leisure to think over his disappointments, when he was suffering physically and mentally, he bore his burden with patience and resignation.

     ✿   ✿   ✿   ✿   ✿

I come now to his religion; the thing which explains him and holds together the qualities that made up his character. Belloc was sceptical by temperament. He did not accept the Catholic Faith because it was a comforting belief, but because he was convinced that it was the Truth. His reason had won what Pascal calls its greatest victory, the surrender to reality. But it will no doubt surprise many who have read or been told that he, in his championship of the Faith, was invariably arrogant and intolerant—it will surprise them to hear that he disliked and despised violent methods as a means of convincing an opponent. Logical argument, close-knit, was his weapon. One obituarist foolishly called him a bigot; that is, an irrational enthusiast. Belloc knew, and sympathized with, the difficulties of the unbeliever, and often provided him with better material for debate than the unbeliever had discovered for himself. It was by the appeal to reason and to intelligence that he sought to persuade. He wrote of immortality:

> There is no man who has closely inquired upon this, and there is none who has troubled himself and admitted a reasonable anxiety upon it, who has not well retained the nature of despair. Those who approach their fellow-beings with assertion and with violence in such a matter, affirming their discovery, their conviction, or their acquired certitude, do an ill service to their kind. It is not thus that the last things should be approached, nor the most tremendous problem which man is doomed to envisage, be propounded and solved. Ah! the long business of this world! The way in which your deepest love goes up in nothingness and breaks away, and the way in which the strongest and the most continuous element of your dear self is dissipated, and fails you in some moment; if I do not understand these things in a man, nor comprehend how the turn of the years can obscure or obliterate a man's consciousness of what is and should be, then I act in brute ignorance, or, what is much worse, in lack of charity.[1]

Belloc had certitude. No writer of his time used rhetoric more majestically. But when he sought to convince, it was by hard prose. He was himself completely assured and satisfied in the matter of religion, but he never made the mistake of acting or talking as though his own impregnable convictions, his personal certitude, were proof of anything. Nor, though he was a man of strong emotions, particularly where his religion was concerned, did he talk of those emotions to anyone who might misunderstand him; to anyone who might imagine that he thought some emotional experience a valid argument. The beauty of many voices singing, the grandeur of the Gothic, sunlight through the windows of Chartres, the darkness and mystery of Spanish churches—all these moved him deeply, and they moved him not only because he responded to

[1] "On Immortality," in *On Something*. (Dutton; 1931.)

beauty, but because they were a frame for the Truth, and because the Church wisely uses beauty to minister to our hunger.

When it came to explaining his religion or attacking its opponents, it should be remembered that he was usually dealing with antagonists who were urged more by a mixture of ignorance and distaste than by rational disagreement. That is why his repetitions and his emphasis became tiresome to some. He was prepared and well equipped to debate with an intelligent opponent who knew what the Catholic Church is but could not accept its claims; nor did he ever assume that what was so clear to him must be equally clear to other people. But the Catholic apologist has to labour against people whom no amount of logical exposition will convince, and must be forever correcting, as publicly as possible, the popular misconceptions which pullulate today.

It was in his writings on religion and history that the aggressiveness which so many resented was most apparent. His religion was the thing for which he cared most, and his perpetual attack was a policy deliberately adopted. He had grown up in an England in which the Catholics had inherited a tradition of the defensive, and as he said: "An ingrained habit of the defensive is the prime condition of defeat. There is no such thing as a defensive battle or a defensive campaign, save in the sense that we may begin on the defensive, but only with the fixed object of turning to the offensive at the right moment."[1] And he believed that the enemies of the Church drew their strength, not from the merits of their case, but from the state of mind of their Catholic opponents. He therefore determined that it was time for a counter-offensive, "because the weight of historical argument is now on our side." He saw, as so

[1] "The Counter-Attack Through History," in *Essays of a Catholic Layman.* (Macmillan: 1931.)

often, the position as a soldier sees a field upon which a
battle is to be fought, and the first essential for the Catholic army was to forget the old habit of feeling inferior to
the enemy, to acquire the mentality of the offensive, and
to attack repeatedly. It was a question of *moral.*

In his private life he never made a parade of his religion.
He liked to begin the day with Mass, whenever that was
possible, but those who, being without experience of the
Catholic world, expected pietism, or even piety, were disappointed. He was more likely to shock them by a jovially
disrespectful way of talking about religious matters. To
Catholics, who are at home in the Church, this familiarity,
which is met with all over Europe, is a commonplace. It is
like a man criticizing the mother he loves, or making fun
of her. But there could be no doubt about the strength of
his faith. His religion satisfied both his intellect and his
emotions. The Church explained to him the purpose of
human life, and solved for him the riddle of human folly
and suffering. Often in his writing, not so often in his talk,
he permitted a glimpse into the depths of his nature, and
when he spoke of solemn things, one was aware of the part
his religion played in his life. He always, for instance, insisted upon the importance of all the traditional observ-
ances connected with the great Feasts of the Church, especially in times of change. In the essay called "A Remaining Christmas" he revealed what reassurance and comfort
he himself drew from the practice of his religion.

> Not only death (which shakes and rends all that is human
> in us, creating a monstrous separation and threatening the
> soul with isolation which destroys)—not only death, but
> that accompaniment of mortality which is a perpetual series
> of lesser deaths and is called change, is challenged, chained,
> and put in its place by unaltered and successive acts of
> seasonable regard for loss and dereliction and mutability.
> The threats of despair, remorse, necessary expiation, weari-

ness almost beyond bearing, dull repetition of things apparently fruitless, unnecessary and without meaning, estrangement, the misunderstanding of mind by mind, forgetfulness, which is a false alarm, grief and repentance, which are true ones, but of a sad company, young men perished in battle before their parents had lost vigour in age, the perils of sickness in the body and even in the mind, anxiety, honour harassed, all the bitterness of living—become part of a large business which may lead to Beatitude. For they are all connected in the memory with holy day after holy day, year by year, binding the generations together, carrying on even in this world, as it were, the life of the dead and giving corporate substance, permanence and stability, without the symbol of which (at least) the vast increasing burden of life might at last conquer us and be no longer borne.[1]

The well-instructed Catholic attaches the highest importance to a full family life. Belloc, both in his writings and in his talk, expressed his conviction that, in a rapidly changing society, the preservation of family ties had become more than ever necessary to a sane way of living. He took his duties as a father seriously, and had imposed a rigid discipline while his children were young. All healthy children resent discipline, but when they grow up, and have families of their own, they realize the wisdom of their parents. The Bellocs had lost their mother when they were young, and they were wild children, who had to be kept in hand. As they grew up, they understood the affection and ceaseless care which had restrained their ebullience. There were, as there are in all families, misunderstandings, sorrows, disappointments, separations. As the children went away from home and passed into the world he saw as much of them as he could and helped them to the limit of his resources, advising them out of his experience of life, and gathering them round him at King's Land whenever it

[1] *A Conversation with an Angel, and other Essays.* (Harper: 1929.)

was possible. Of his relations with Peter and Stella Belloc I can speak with knowledge, both from my own observations and from the correspondence which Stella Belloc has allowed me to see. He was always ready with sympathy and practical help in those difficulties which confront a young married couple, and would go to endless trouble to do a service for them, or for Reginald and Eleanor Jebb. He thought a great deal about their future, and he made their anxieties his own, as a matter of course. He shirked nothing that he thought his duty, and would have considered himself dishonoured if he had not made sacrifices of time and labour for them. But he went far beyond duty. When his grandchildren were born, he lost no occasion of showing his love, and that tenderness which surprised so many when they met it for the first time—a tenderness which those who knew his poetry were prepared for. The innocence of children, as he once said to me, "moves me to tears," and I have seen a letter written by him to little Gabrielle Elodie Belloc, which ends, "Remember my name when you say your prayers." Fortunate is he for whom children pray.

    ❋   ❋   ❋   ❋   ❋

When Belloc came into a room he changed that room. Even those who did not know him were made aware of the mysterious force which we call personality. He imposed himself by his presence, and without effort. He never in his life made a show of being a celebrity, never attempted to draw attention to himself. The black clothes carelessly worn, the intelligent face, the direct, unwavering, penetrating glance of the eyes attracted notice, but the deeper impression one received was of power, of energy under command, of dignity, of distinction. He was a many-sided man, but beneath the apparent contradictions and complexities of his character he was all of one piece, and easier to understand if you treated him as a simple man. There was in him no trace of hypocrisy or humbug, nor even of affectation. He was a loyal friend and a dangerous enemy. Since his life was ruled by certain iron convictions, his response to any given circumstances could be anticipated. In what touched his honour he permitted no compromise, made no concession. He conceived it to be his duty to bear witness to the truth, not hesitatingly or quietly, but with enthusiasm, and in the face of the world. Though his campaigns isolated him and destroyed his peace of mind, he struck no noble attitude, but complained incessantly in a humorous manner which endeared him to a very large circle of friends. Repeated attack, with the odds always against him, suited his virile character, but it was also the outcome of a planned strategy. He was aggressive both by temperament and by the conditions of the time in which he lived. And it was not always realized that his assault on the modern world was disinterested, in the sense that there was for himself no guerdon but the consciousness of having kept faith with himself. His work for the Church, for the restoration of Europe, for social justice, for the independence and liberty of men without property, for cleaner public life, for the Catholic schools, for the exposure of Whig history—all the long list of arduous tasks which he undertook, brought him only unpopularity, loss of income, broken health, and a growing embitterment. It would have been easy to give in, to tell himself that he had made the effort, that he had put into it all his strength, all his genius, all his enthusiasm, and that it was clearly of no avail. But he was not of those who surrender; which is one of the things nobody could doubt after an hour in his company.

Often in London, in the midst of his life's turmoil, when he was writing three or four books, speaking on platforms up and down England, embroiled in controversy, and

turning out weekly essays and miscellaneous articles, he
would utter a great cry of exasperation. That cry recalled
to me Danton's *"Je suis saoul des hommes,"* or Desmoulins
asking, "Where are my fields of Guise?", or Saint-Just
telling his friend in the tavern at Laon the kind of life he
longed for if ever he could escape from public affairs.
Belloc felt profoundly a double exile. He could look back
on a full family life in his own home, with a wife and
growing children; and that was finished. But there was
also a sense of exile from which none of us escape. For all
his capacity for enjoyment, he returned again and again,
in his talk, but more often in his writing, to that theme. At
sea his thoughts were often on the last harbour of all, and
on land he was haunted by the vision of that City which
is round the bend in every road. These longings appear
constantly in his work, and when he is writing of such
things he is writing out of the depths of his nature. His
belief in immortality and in all the doctrines of the Church
sustained him to the end, because it was not simply a
soothing emotion, but a reasoned belief which his intellect
could accept.

It is a commonplace to say that a literary man is never
like his writing; that when you meet a man whose writing
you have admired and enjoyed, you always are disappointed. Belloc was like his writing. When you talked to
him, or when you read him, you noted his zest for life, his
appetite for conflict, his swift changes of mood, his orderly
method of thought, his certitudes, his sense of fun, his
hatred of injustice. His very manner of speech was often
echoed in his writing—with all kinds of parenthesis and
afterthought thrown out noisily and impudently. But one
who expected to conduct with him a literary conversation on the usual lines was doomed to disappointment.
People discovered astonishing gaps in his reading, for he
never pretended to have read a book if he had not read it.

The writers he talked of most, during the years I knew him, were Homer and Catullus, Swift and Rabelais. He was always quoting Horace and Ronsard, and always re-reading Molière, *Vathek* and *Rasselas*. Of his contemporaries he read little: of Chesterton and Baring he had the highest opinion, and of the prose (but not the ideas) of Wells. "Pitcher" (Arthur Binstead), Wodehouse, Ernest Bramah and the *Diary of a Nobody* he praised perpetually, and among modern poets, A. E. Housman, Yeats and Ruth Pitter. His excitement when he discovered something that he thought good was boyish. He could not rest until he had told his discovery to all his friends, and Maurice Baring has recorded that Belloc would exclaim, "Why was I never told about this?" when shown some piece of writing which he at once admired.

Belloc's confident and overbearing manner in the assertion of his opinions was often the outcome of impatience with unintelligent criticism. With intelligent criticism he was always prepared to debate, since he delighted in the clash of controversy, and was a man of far too great sincerity to override reasonable opposition by mere loud asseveration. What bored him, and ended by annoying him, was a long-winded and pointless discussion or a muddled argument. The processes of his own thought were orderly, and the idea of simply talking and getting nowhere did not appeal to him. Many people resented his habit of making some pronouncement, in the middle of an aimless discussion, with the air of "That settles it. There is no more to be said."

I remember an occasion when a roomful of people were talking about genius. Dr. Johnson's absurd definition was, as always, quoted, and various other suggestions were made. Suddenly Belloc said, "Genius is the ability to think in a very large number of categories," and at once changed the subject. He had another disconcerting habit which irritated people. He would pick out the weak point in an argument, and by following it to its logical conclusion, expose its ludicrousness. The good-humoured way in which this was done sometimes added to the irritation. One might think that one who was so masterful and pugnacious would have had no use for the shy and the diffident, unless they simply allowed themselves to be bullied and cowed. This was by no means the case. Among the friends he loved best was Tommy Pope, one of those self-effacing, meek men who seem to be helpless in the face of the world. Belloc saw the simplicity of Pope and loved him for it, but if Belloc trod on any of his convictions, or seemed to be talking nonsense, Pope defended himself with spirit in the one case, and gurgled with scornful laughter in the other. They made an odd couple, but their friendship was solid and enduring, and serves as an example of an unexpected facet of Belloc. He was always attached to goodness, to quiet sincerity and to the uncomplicated.

As a companion he was more stimulating than any man I have known. This was due not merely to his ability to be interesting on any and every subject, but also to the independence of his thought, and to a peculiar way of expressing himself. His enjoyment of life was infectious, and though he was, as I shall show in the course of this Memoir, a saddened and disappointed man, his nature was so robust that his noisy gaiety was a legend in his lifetime. Flashes of that gaiety lasted to the end of his life, when, as a very old man, with memory impaired and increasing physical infirmity, he showed the strength of his character and the high quality of his courage. There were certain circumstances connected with his last years, a burden additional to his ill-health, which had to be borne. He did not speak of these matters, though day by day, and every day, they challenged his fortitude and increased his unhappiness. Yet, my last memories of him in his study at

King's Land, though they are of longer silences than I had been accustomed to, and of anxiety for him, are also of laughter and song. And because I count it among the good fortunes of my life to have been the friend of such a man, I have tried, in the pages that follow, to leave some memorial, however inadequate, of Hilaire Belloc.

2

THE RODMELL DAYS

The traveller who comes through lewes and southover on his way to Newhaven rounds a corner as he leaves Southover, and sees before him the bare Downs, and to his left the broad flats of the Ouse, broken by a solitary hillock. As he follows the road, he passes the ruins of Lewes Priory. Across the levels Caburn and Itford guard, on either side, the gateway of the Vale of Glynde, and, more distant, the great promontory of Firle Beacon juts out into the Weald. The road runs to the foot of the Downs, and then turns westward, with the Downs on its right, and on its left the water-meadows, or the Brooks, as they are called locally. At the edge of these meadows the traveller will notice occasional very small villages. They have changed little since the time when they were sheep-farms, with a rough track connecting one with the other. The traffic which goes by on the main road does not disturb them, and they are unknown to many motorists who use that road to reach the Channel boats. Today these villages still preserve an air of remoteness; there has been some building, notably on Mill Hill, above Rodmell, but the general aspect of the countryside is unchanged. Rodmell, about three miles from Lewes, is reached by a sharp turning from the main road, or by a path across the fields. The little lane, on either side of which the houses of the village are built, fades out in the meadows at the northern end of the village. The Ouse is about half a mile away. A few minutes' walk southwards brings you to the top of Mill Hill, and to the rolling downland, with the sea four miles away. It is a country of secret combes, and steadings which are hidden until you stand above them on the lip of a steep fall. There are no woods, but only patches of gorse, and occasional groups of trees for windbreaks. Telscombe, right down in a little bowl, is the only village on the way to the sea, but the fringe of building on the coast is continuous now. Where there were two coastguards' cottages thirty years ago, there is a settlement, and the new "estates" are spreading inland, eroding the fields and the slopes. But the villages under the northern edge of the Downs are almost untouched by development.

In the year 1922 I had come to live in a cottage at the northern end of Rodmell, and on an October morning of that year I was in the house of a friend, when a motor-bicycle came down the lane. It stopped suddenly outside the house with a rattle, a crash, and what sounded like an explosion. That explosion continued for the next twenty years of my life.

I rose to my feet, intending to find out what had happened, but before I reached the door, there burst into the room a broad-shouldered, thick-set young man. His clothes and his rumpled brown hair looked as though he had slept in a haystack. He wore an enormous pair of riding-boots, old riding-breeches, and a nondescript coat, but the thing my eye fixed on was a neat little dark moustache, which seemed ludicrously out of place on that large, beaming face. The young man, whose eyes danced with laughter, appeared to realize the incongruity, for, with a Meissonier gesture, he plucked off the moustache, and stuffed it into his coat pocket. He then introduced himself to me as Sir Almeric Fitzroy, in a voice that rang through the house, and brought a number of people into the room. Someone asked where he had got his boots, and he answered in a quieter and graver tone, "I cut them off a dead man in the road." He then recited some lines of a sonnet, sang a verse of the immortal song called "The Winged Horse," and threw himself into a chair. I asked who he was, and was told Peter Belloc. For the rest of the day, on through the night, and into the small hours of the morning, we made up for some of the time we had lost before our meeting. I think each of us knew that only death would separate us, and he became my closest friend. Twenty years later he was a Captain in the Royal Marines, and he died on active service in 1941.

The house in which this meeting took place belonged to James Murray Allison, the remarkable Australian who, after a wild and adventurous youth, came to England and quickly made his name in the advertising world. It was he who, while owner of *Land and Water*, had the perspicacity to engage Hilaire Belloc to write a weekly article on the war. After a first meeting at King's Land, Belloc's home at Shipley, the two men became close friends. Allison had settled at Rodmell, where he had a sheep-farm, and it was round him and his beautiful and gracious wife that the life of the village centred. They kept open house, and the young Bellocs and their friends were frequent visitors. Allison was never happier than when surrounded by a crowd of noisy young people— "I like to fill my house with Red Indians," he said. For Hilaire Belloc, Hill Farm was a kind of port of call on his frequent journeys to and from France, Newhaven being only four miles away. He was godfather to the Allisons' little boy, who was to lose his life in the Dieppe raid. Edward Shanks, who owed so much to Allison's encouragement, and Clennell Wilkinson, the biographer and journalist, also lived in the village. There was an ancient church, a small shop, and an inn, and the population, I suppose, was about two hundred. Within a few minutes you were on the Downs, and you could walk or ride for miles without meeting anyone. The air was nearly always bright and clear, and all this land was unfenced, an inexhaustible playground. The conformation of the hills hid the coastal building estates until you were a mile or so from the sea.

Tout le monde savait chanter. Le chant n'était pas, chez les Baudouin, la manifestation d'un art savant, c'était un des phénomènes élémentaires de la vie. Duhamel's description, in *Suzanne et les Jeunes Hommes,* of the happy Baudoin household, always makes me think of Allison's house at Rodmell. Everyone sang continually, before meals, during meals and after meals. We sang our own songs, Belloc's songs, and everybody else's songs, and the outburst was always completely spontaneous. As one starts a conversation in easy and familiar surroundings, so we would start a song. Often I watched the amazement of those who were unaccustomed to such riotous gaiety. Some would forget their shyness and join in, others would listen as to a performance, and I remember one occasion of cold disapproval. Occasionally the rough and ragged choruses would die down and something very moving would happen, as when Elsie Allison sang "The Bonny Earl of Moray" or "You Wear the Morning Like Your Dress," in her deep, soft voice. Allison himself had a store of ridiculous songs and ridiculous stories. He was the only man I ever knew who could tell an enormously long story without boring his listeners. Nobody knew better how to build up details, prolong suspense, and then spring the surprise of a preposterous climax. It always amazed me that this boyish man, who was a bird-watcher, a painter and a writer of verse and prose, had concealed about him the patience and the self-discipline to become advertising manager of *The Times* and, later, of the *Daily Telegraph*. Seeing him at his own table, you could not believe that he took anything seriously.

I was an enthusiastic admirer of Belloc's books, and everything I heard of him at Rodmell made me anxious to meet him. I had been told, however, that he did not take readily to strangers, and I was therefore surprised when I received a letter from Peter Belloc saying that they would like me to come to King's Land for Christmas. Peter Belloc told me quite frankly that he had had considerable difficulty with his father, before he would finally consent to invite someone of whom he knew nothing. We went down from London together, and I was warned to expect a cold reception. The reception was cold, but extremely courteous. Dinner was over, and Belloc was in the stone-flagged, oak-panelled dining-room with his old friend Somers Cocks. He was at the head of an ancient refectory table,[1] and when we came in he gave me a direct look, and shook hands with that little bow of his. He said, "What will you drink, Mr. Martin?", motioned me to a seat at his side, and began to talk about the Stane Street, various theories of the surveying methods of the Romans, and the ignorance of the dons. I drank my beer out of a great pewter flagon, and presently heard that phrase so well known to all his friends. "Mr. Martin," he said, "I must know your plans." I, who had made no plans, probably looked surprised, for he went on, "You can stay as long as you like,

---

[1] This table, three hundred years old, had once been in one of the Oxford colleges. Belloc bought it in the year of his marriage, 1896.

or go as soon as you like, but I must know your plans." This
military precision was so foreign to my own nature that,
with anyone less formidable, I should have laughed, and
made a jest of it. But he produced a time-table, and I chose
a day and a train at random. He was satisfied. The "staff-
work," as he always called it, was finished, and we settled
down for the night.

On the next day, Christmas Eve, I had an opportunity
to get my bearings. I had never been in Shipley, which is
still something of a lost village; a few old houses and cottages, dominated by the King's Land mill, with the line of
the Downs to the north. The house, with many gables, and
with modern additions, has a fourteenth-century core, and
is all brick and oak. It faces west, and between its front
and the open fields runs one of those old tracks that were
long ago the only means of communication in the forest of
the Weald. The house was—and is still—lit only by candles
and oil lamps. The most striking part of it is the stone-
flagged hall, panelled, and with a very high roof. It has a
huge open hearth, and a staircase which must be as old as
the house leads up to a gallery, where stands a statue of
Our Lady, in wood.

I had seen Belloc on three occasions before this. He had
come to Harrow to lecture on Waterloo when I was a boy
at the school, and I had heard him lecture on Alsace and
Lorraine when I was in the Army during the first war.
Later on I had seen him walking along the Strand with his
friend Tommy Pope, and had been struck by that peculiar
walk I have mentioned. I now had leisure to observe him.
He looked considerably older than his fifty-two years. Had
I known nothing about him, it would have been impossible to "place" him. The black clothes, black tie, and old-
fashioned, stiff, stick-up collar made him look like the
Frenchmen of my boyhood. But the ruddy complexion
and the broad, square shoulders and massive body gave

him the air of an English farmer. His eyes were blue, and
when spoken to or speaking he would move his head
sharply, and look straight at you, as though he were not
only carrying on a conversation but reading a character.
His greying hair, cut *en brosse,* accentuated the round
head, but the most arresting feature was the magnificent
jaw. A certain kind of sardonic smile, which weighed
down his mouth at the corners, emphasized the strength
of his face. It was the face of a fighter, as was the manner
of speech. I never saw anyone who looked less like a man
of letters. His voice was another surprise, being a clear
tenor, not loud, but very penetrating. He talked quickly
and with an extraordinary facility, and he could never be
dull because, whatever his subject, he could never resist
highly amusing parentheses. He had no small talk, and
took for granted, in any company in which he found himself, a high degree of intelligence and an amount of varied
knowledge which flattered some and frightened others,
and I think that most of the people who accused him of
monopolizing the conversation would have made a pretty
poor job of arguing with him. Very often his talk was
monologue either because his hearers had nothing to contribute, or, if they had, were content to listen.

It was the custom of the house at Christmas to hear the
three Masses in the chapel above the dining-room, but this
year Father Vincent McNabb was unable to come, and so
we were to go to West Grinstead for the midnight Mass.
But before this there was much to be done. Soon after
darkness had fallen on Christmas Eve the children of the
village arrived, with their parents and relatives, and
plentiful food and drink were provided for them. They
were then entertained by a magic lantern, after which
they were brought to the hall, where there was a tall
Christmas tree, with little coloured candles and presents
among its branches. Each child was given a present, and

then a sixpence. After this they all sang songs and played games—the traditional songs and games of this part of Sussex. When they grew tired of this, they were taken to the Crib, and, gathered round it, they, their parents and the rest of us sang carols. A large, jovial man with a tremendous voice led the singing, and I was told that he was the miller.

When the children had gone home we had a collation, and then drove to West Grinstead, with Belloc himself at the wheel of the Ford, wearing a bowler hat. As we went along the frosty lanes we sang the *Adeste Fideles* in chorus —Peter, his married sister Eleanor, and I were the passengers, Reginald Jebb, Eleanor's husband, being laid up with influenza, and Hilary and Elizabeth Belloc away from home. All this made a memorable Christmas for me, who had only been received into the Church that summer. On Christmas Day we had one of those prolonged feasts for which King's Land was renowned, and I found my host less formidable. The eating and drinking went on far into the afternoon. For the rest of the day we talked and sang songs. Shortly after midnight, on a sudden impulse, Peter and I set out on foot for Rodmell, going across fields and by lanes south-eastwards until we came to the Downs. Sleep overcame us somewhere between Plumpton and Offham, and we lay down for an hour in an old cart which stood under an open shed. We arrived at Rodmell in the early morning, and roused the Allison household, every member of which cursed us individually and by name. We roamed about, and at night Belloc arrived in his car. He sang a great many songs, said, "If the young knew what was ahead of them, they wouldn't want to live," told amusing stories, castigated the "rich," the professional politicians, the Press, and stimulated the uproar of happiness whenever it showed signs of dying down through sheer fatigue. A moment of unwonted quiet was broken by Belloc with that excellent ditty:

> Am I a man or am I a mouse?
>   Am I hedger or a dodger?
> I should bloody well like to know
>   Who's running this damned show—
> Is it me or the top floor lodger?

Somewhere about midnight Belloc and Peter left in the Ford car, and quiet Night came into her own at last.

❖   ❖   ❖   ❖   ❖

Early in 1923 Belloc went to America, and came back by way of France. Allison and I met him at Newhaven and brought him back to Rodmell. I had, at first, the unflattering impression that he had no idea who I was. He treated me with distant courtesy; but later on, I corrected my first impression, and realized that he did not much care for me —which was a disappointment to me, who had very much wanted to know him better. I saw him occasionally after this at Rodmell, and the disapproval seemed to be less. The fact that he ever accepted me as a friend needs some explanation. It was in 1923 that the family life at King's Land was broken up. Peter left for Spain, to go to sea in a Spanish ship, and Hilary, his elder brother, went to America. The dispersion of the family left Belloc very lonely, and he spent most of his time in London, returning home at the week-ends. He had lost in a short space of time several close friends among his contemporaries. George Wyndham in 1913, the year before his wife's death, and then Raymond Asquith, Lord Lucas, Cecil Chesterton. Philip Kershaw and John Phillimore he was soon to lose. I was company for him, because I was always within call, and extremely idle. I was young, and so was well able to accommodate myself to the demands which his energy made on those who associated with him. I began to meet him more in London, and often went down to Shipley with him. He had what the French call *la bougeotte*. He could not remain still in one place, and much of the time was spent, at week-ends, in driving all over the county, looking in at one house or another. But the most memorable part of those days for me was that moment after dinner at King's Land, when he would place a candlestick on each side of him at the dining-table, and play patience. As he played, he would talk, hour after hour, while I drank my port and listened, occasionally leading him on to develop some point. And that was the best, the fullest, the most creative talk (to use a phrase Robert Lynd applied to his conversation) I ever heard in my life.

The subject was anything that came into his head: the breakdown of our civilization, history, economics, politics, travel, military campaigns, the sea, physical science, poetry, wine, religion, the English character, international affairs. One thing would lead to another, and the whole would be seasoned with songs and jests and other digressions. It was not merely the variety of the talk that was so amazing. It came bubbling and boiling out of his richly stored mind like a dozen of his own essays; ribaldry, wit, irony, tomfoolery, all mixed with profound wisdom. I understood why his more uproarious essays read like a man talking at the top of his voice. For here were those unexpected asides, those classical tags. Here were the original twists of phrase, the odd bits of scholarship, the outrageous exaggerations, the flashes of poetry. A kind of boyish exuberance was blended with cynicism and ferocious satire. The greatness of the man was more apparent even than it is in his books.

His versatility was as striking in his talk as in his books. I can imagine a man coming new to his books, and finding it difficult to believe that *The Servile State* and *Marie Antoinette*, and the Sonnets and *The Green Overcoat*

and *Esto Perpetua* and the light verse were by one and
the same author. There would be equal surprise in hearing
him talk well, and within an hour, on Homer, on the Ice
Age, on Music Halls, and on Arianism. There was no
artifice in his conversation, no striving for cleverness, no
self-satisfaction when he chose an apt metaphor or said a
witty thing. His talk was never the set-piece, with ordered
periods. What made it so entertaining, apart from his unusual opinions, his individual approach to a question, was
its spontaneity. Most of what he said was said colloquially,
in his own vigorous everyday language, with a plentiful
use of slang. Often I have heard him begin to discuss an
historical character in some such words as: "There was a
filthy beast in human form called ——." Then would follow the principal incidents in the man's career, related
with comic exaggeration. He said once to a startled man
who had made a cautious remark: "Oh, that's Nominalism.
The Nominalists said there was no such thing as a river;
only a lot of water." And into a solemn discussion on "the
survival of the fittest" he barged with: "Oh, I know all
about that. If you throw a baby into a mill-race it will
drown, but a strong swimmer may save himself." His contribution to a conversation about music was: "A perfectly
foul woman often has a lovely voice. That shows how
powerful the Devil is."

In London we used to meet for a meal, or in a bodega,
to drink the white port of which he was so fond. A favourite meeting-place was the Red Lion in Poppins Court,
off Fleet Street. Sir John Squire had his *London Mercury*
offices near by, and the public house was always crammed
with writers and journalists. In those days I shared a flat
in the Middle Temple with Edward Shanks. Every day
a lunch was prepared for us by a housekeeper, but not
once during our tenancy of the flat did we return to eat it,

and I remember the lean young J. B. Priestley saying that
the trouble with the whole lot of us was that we never did
any work. That remark certainly did not apply to Belloc;
but the mystery of when and how he did his work was an
intriguing one. He would come in, and without any prelude but a hard, sharp cough, launch out on a tirade
against the abominations of modern life or the imbecility
of the politicians. Being without a particle of affectation,
he was completely unaware of the attention he attracted
by the power of his voice, the unusual nature of what he
was saying, and his striking appearance. He would say to
the man who happened to be next to him at the bar:
"What do you think will happen to this country? Will
there be a sudden collapse or a slow decay?" He himself
thought that a slow process of decay was ahead of us, and
he would give his reasons: "Point one . . . Point two . . .
Point three . . ." Sometimes he and I would go to the
London Mercury office, and I remember him sitting down
in Squire's room and writing out the sonnet, "Your life is
like a little winter's day," which was to appear in the next
issue, talking and jesting as he wrote it out, in that most
hugger-mugger of editorial offices.

I noticed at this time how he stimulated everybody with
whom he came in contact. He forced you to think. Often
I have heard a man express an obviously second-hand
opinion, and say, in regard to some public question, that
such and such could not be done, or must be done. Belloc
would look straight at him and say "Why not?" or "Why
do you say that?" The man had often not really thought
about the thing at all. I remember once quoting St.
Thomas on prayer, and going off into a long discourse on
the highest form of prayer, which does not concentrate on
the words or the meaning of words. I said that this had
impressed me very much. "Has the idea never occurred

to you," said Belloc, "of lifting up your heart to God?"
I was boring him, so he cut the tedium short.

His rebukes were not always as gentle as that. He was
master of a classical ferocity, as when he said to Ramsay
MacDonald: "Take care lest I make you immortal with an
epigram." The method he would use for crushing foolishness depended on his mood. An American who was lunching with us expected that a lover of wine would hold his
glass up to the light, sniff, taste, roll round the tongue and
go through all the prescribed ritual with an ordinary table
wine. When Belloc took a deep draught, the American
said, in a horrified tone: "Mr. Belloc! You! The great con-
noisseur! You! To gulp your wine like that!" "It's all alco-
hol to me," said Belloc. Again, a certain society pest whom
he did not know was plaguing him to lunch at her house.
She ended by wiring him a pressing invitation. He replied:
"Just up from the south just off to the north." I once took
the chair for him and Chesterton at a Distributist meeting in the Strand, and at the end of the meeting questions
were fired at the platform. The good-natured, easy-going
Chesterton would have sat there all night answering even
the silliest questions. Belloc whispered loudly to me,
after a while: "We can't go on like this. Stop them. You're
chairman, you can stop them." He was fond of telling the
story of the poet who gave a reading of his verse. A jolly
fellow at the back of the hall, after listening to the dron-
ing as patiently as he could, thought he detected signs of
the ordeal coming to an end. To hearten the rest of the
audience, he cried out: "Courage, lads! I see land!"

He was even more restless in London than at home. His
distaste for loneliness was increasing, and he liked to have
his whole day planned, with engagements from morning
till night, and in between these engagements he would dictate articles and books and essays at top speed, and tele-

phone to a score of people. His passion for the telephone was a family joke. He would never have one in his home, but "I must telephone" were words which, in a favourite phrase of his, "Sprang unbidden to his lips" on all occasions. In the middle of a lunch or a dinner he always had to telephone. If there was no telephone handy, he sent telegrams later on. I never knew him go anywhere on the chance of meeting a friend. He must always know time and place, and was always most precise in giving information on his own movements. I have among my papers a number of telegrams and letters making appointments, many of them as detailed as the orders for a military operation. Very often, while wandering about abroad, he would work out a complicated itinerary, day by day, and then write to me a good while in advance, giving the time and place he would expect to meet me on his return, and instructions for a reply which would catch him in some town of France or Spain or even farther afield, on a given date. I became familiar, at a later period, with this habit. He would drag the *Indicateur Chaix* out of the pocket of his cloak in some restaurant or café, and set to work like a General preparing a campaign, taking immense pains to allow for every possible check to his plans.

Two of the places where we used to lunch have disappeared. One was a sausage-shop in Fleet Street. You saw the sausages cooking in the window, and they were genuine sausages, without that metallic tang which is now a masterpiece of the chemist's art. It was a cheap, rough sort of place, and today would be called unhygienic. But if it existed today there would be chromium stools and white-coated attendants and loathsome food. The other place was under the viaduct at Ludgate Hill—famous also for its sausages, but with a less happy-go-lucky atmosphere. Archie Macdonell frequently joined us there. He was a cousin of an old Oxford friend of Belloc, Sir Philip Macdonell, and in his book, *England, their England,* he immortalized the famous Rodmell cricket match.

❄   ❄   ❄   ❄   ❄

Every year Sir John Squire used to bring his team, the Invalids, to play the village, and this was one of the great occasions in the happy-go-lucky life at Rodmell. So many people came and went during the day that it was difficult to know who was playing in the match and who was not. It was light-hearted cricket of the best kind. The match was played in a field with a magnificent view over the Brooks, with Caburn dominating the Vale of Glynde. Belloc came occasionally and told improbable tales of his feats on the cricket field. During one match he spoke of his book *Europe and the Faith.* "What Faith is that?" asked a clergyman. "The Faith of Europe," said Belloc, thereby ending that conversation. The village inn did a roaring trade on these occasions, and you could never be sure that there were eleven people fielding, or that the next man in would not have to be hastily summoned from the inn. I remember a young man, who was playing in the match, bursting in upon our drinking, with a very anxious face. He had been sent to find someone who should have been ready to go to bat. He glanced round, and then said breathlessly: "The wickets are falling like rain." A low growl answered him. The innkeeper had the admirable name of Malthouse, and his cure for all human ills was "a drop of the old and an onion cut up." Describing a fox he had seen, he said: "There he was, bothering along the road, as though tomorrow would do." I once made the mistake of talking politics with him. He said "Politics. Politicians. You know how it is, you see a slimy pond, with a lot of insects swimming round in it, and you go off to bed, and next morning, there they all are, still mucking round in the dirty water. That's politics. That's politicians for you."

The central point of the match was the lunch which Allison gave in one of his great barns, and one did not need to be fond of cricket to try to get into one team or the other, and if that failed, to slip in as a hanger-on. Our captain asked me once if I ever played. I told him I used to be a pure slogger, but had not touched a bat since 1914. When I went in I had to face a very fast bowler, Colin Hurry, and he tempted me with a slow ball, which I hit clean out of the ground. A great cheer went up from friend and foe alike. I ran half-way up the pitch to the next ball, and was caught on the boundary.

After the match the merriment used to go on far into the night, and on one occasion there was a complaint made by a very respectable spinster that she had found dozens of empty bottles on her doorstep. For there were quiet people in that tempestuous village, including a man who objected to one of Allison's cows, which had strayed, and had "poked its head in at my window. Imagine my feelings." "Imagine the cow's feelings," said Allison. It was also told that Clennell Wilkinson, whose emphatic manner of speaking was carried into the smallest of small talk, once said "Good morning" so heartily and loudly to a shy lady that she fainted.

❧   ❧   ❧   ❧   ❧

Allison was an excellent companion for Belloc, because his great admiration for him never prevented him making fun of his idiosyncrasies, and laughing at his "staff-work." I think it was the genuine simplicity and goodness in Allison that appealed to Belloc most strongly, and, of course, his unfailing gaiety. Allison's warmth and generosity went far beyond the keeping of open house. It was unsafe to admire anything he possessed, for he would at once give it to you. George Mair came to me in great distress one day. He had been struck by a picture in Allison's flat in the

Temple. "He took it down and gave it to me," he said. "What ought I to do? I don't know him at all well." I assured him that this was always happening, and that it made Allison happy to be able to make other people happy. Belloc was particularly impressed by Allison's response, when they travelled together abroad, to landscape and architecture, and to history. He expected that a man to whom Europe was new and unfamiliar, and one so much of whose life was passed in the world of newspapers, would respond as he was expected to respond, would judge things by what he had read or heard of them. But it was not so. Allison, as Belloc said: "Saw what was in front of him, and not some image conveyed to him by previous reading." For nothing made Belloc more impatient than a second-hand conventional opinion. When you looked at a building or a range of mountains, read a book, went to a play or drank a bottle of wine, he expected you to say what you thought, not what you imagined you were expected to think.

Belloc would arrive in Rodmell in what he called his "self-moving vehicle." His arrival was always expected. He would never take anyone by surprise, and did not want anyone to take him by surprise in his own home. He would probably have written or wired asking if his visit was convenient. Then he would write to confirm it. He would then ring up from somewhere on the way, saying he was twenty minutes late or ten minutes early, or whatever it might be. He would enter the house shouting: "My children, I must telephone. I can't eat anything but bread and ham. Or can I have eggs and bacon?" He always addressed a company, of whatever age, as "my children." He would be wearing a cloak over his black clothes, the pockets stuffed with French and English newspapers, and in one of them a flask of port for the journey. Into this pocket he would cram his round black hat. While waiting at the telephone

he would tell some amusing story about a politician, or discuss some bit of research he had done for a book. The
telephoning finished, he would begin to sing or to recite
some verse he had lately composed. Then he would say,
out of the blue, something like, "How do you suppose the
Scandinavian pirates dragged their boats up the shingle?"
and then develop his own theory. And one of the things he
liked best in Allison was the variety of his interests. Whatever the subject Belloc started, he could always be sure
that Allison would not say, like the rest of us: "I haven't
the slightest idea." He would ask some intelligent question, or formulate some theory of his own. But serious discussion never went on long at Rodmell, because the company was, for the most part, young people. There were
several of the girls with whom Eleanor Belloc had been at
school, and a friend or two of Hilary and Peter. I remember one such, now a respected magistrate, who came to
read quietly in this remote village during his vacation.
After a week of hurlyburly, he and I were sitting in an inn
at Newhaven one evening, when the siren of the Channel
boat sounded. We raced to the harbour, bought tickets for
Dieppe, and walked out to Berneval, of which my father
had been so fond. We had no sleep that day, and we came
back on the Sunday night boat, and wandered to Rodmell
by way of the Downs. My companion announced the next
day that Rodmell was not the ideal place for quiet study,
and he left, never to return.

Among the frequent visitors to Rodmell was Tommy
Pope, the shy, unassuming little man of whom Belloc was
particularly fond. He had a bubbling sense of humour, and
a most attractive helplessness and vagueness, which made
him fall in with anything that was suggested. When he
died, Belloc told me many a time how much he missed
him. Another friend of Allison's was the handsome Scots-
man, James Gunn, one of whose portraits of Belloc now

hangs in the Union at Oxford. At Rodmell Gunn met, and later married, Pauline Miller who, like Peter Belloc's future wife and her sister, had been at school with the Belloc girls, Eleanor and Elizabeth. At Rodmell, again, after a tremendous feast, was announced the engagement of Allison's old friend Count Vanden Heuvel to Katherine O'Leary, who had been Belloc's secretary, and whose sister became my wife. So, as Tchekov (or somebody) said of Gogol, we all came out from under Allison's cloak.

Reginald Jebb, who had married Eleanor Belloc, had a preparatory school at Eridge, and Belloc and I often went over there together. As at Rodmell, there were continual comings and goings of all the friends, and I have often wondered how on earth a schoolmaster contrived to keep his mind on the school in such an unscholastic atmosphere. As the godfather of their first child, a girl, born at their former home in Horsham, I did, on one occasion, show a momentary consideration for the parents. Instead of knocking them up in the middle of the night, when I was wandering about the countryside, I slept in the doorway of a stable, and was found there in the morning by a startled junior master.

I heard Belloc lecture to the school on trigonometry. Few people, I think, realized that he was a considerable mathematician, but you were aware of it when you heard him talk about the technical details of bridges or about squaring the circle. He had the mathematician's eye for a landscape, as well as the poet's, and in his descriptions of military campaigns he always took great pains to work out the details of the movements of troops and guns, and the influence on those movements of the various conditions of weather, fatigue and other accidents, and then to apply the test of common sense and personal experience to his conclusions. He arrived once in Rodmell with a theodolite. He was on his way to survey the field of the battle of

Hastings, and he was full of his subject. As often when he was writing a book, he talked it first, putting forward his own convictions, then setting up the errors he had discovered in the work of other men, and knocking them down. And, as always, nobody could find what he had to say dull, whether they were interested in the subject or not, because his manner of expressing himself was so unusual. It was talk, never a mere lecture. It was rapid, and shot through with flashes of humour and with the odd scraps of slang, which he used so often in his writing as well as in his speech. On this occasion there was a long tirade about Lingard's footnote, and the subsequent use of the word Senlac for Hastings.

Once at Rodmell someone asked him a question about the French Revolution, and he told us how, as a little boy, he had been taken to see Mlle. Montgolfier, who was the daughter of the balloonist, and his father's godmother. She had told him how she had seen the mob going through Paris to attack the Bastille. It was the living chain of memory that impressed him so much. His great sense of the past was nourished by such a memory, and he said to me: "I may tell that story in extreme old age to my son's grandchildren. In *their* extreme old age, they will say they had heard a tale of the Fall of the Bastille from the man it was originally told to—and that link will stretch over more than two centuries." He then sang, in a very delicate, light voice some song of the Court of Louis XVI. "That was how they sang before the Revolution," he said. And then he suddenly bellowed with all the power of his lungs the "Chant du Départ." "That's how they sang when the Revolution came," he said. He went on to talk of the French Army, and of his own days as a gunner. I said that it must have been an odd experience to come from the French Army to Oxford. He said: "Yes. They'd never had a French gunner at Balliol." And he told one of his favourite stories.

There was a very rich and very stupid undergraduate, who found such insuperable difficulty in writing the weekly essay which had to be read to the Master in his study, that he hired a poor clergyman to write his essays for him, at so much a go. One week the task was to discuss Æschylus, Sophocles and Euripides. The young man received his essay from the impoverished cleric, and took it along. Jowett told him to begin. He began: "When one considers the warm humanity of Euripides, the powerful restraint of Æschylus, the iron strength of Bophocles——" The Master held up his hand. "Sophocles, Mr. ——," he said. The young man moved to the window, and held the sheet of paper to the light. "No, Master. Bophocles. It's a capital B. It's quite plain." In telling of his days at Oxford, he never spoke of his Brackenbury scholarship or his successes at the Union, but always of practical jokes and the lighter side of University life; of the "throwing port," a cheap brand kept for throwing about the room, and suchlike things. But he always ended with a diatribe against the unbelievable foolishness of the dons, the more ridiculous of whom, he used to say, walked sideways.

❖   ❖   ❖   ❖   ❖

He loved to hear his own songs sung in chorus, and always insisted that they should be sung in the right way. It was most important, for instance, to sing "Mrs. Rhys" as a mazurka. He told us: "I made it up in a forest in France, on my way to see an eclipse of the sun." The lovely little song: "The Early Morning":

> The moon on the one hand, the dawn on the other:
> The moon is my sister, the dawn is my brother.
> The moon on my left and the dawn on my right.
> My brother, good morning: my sister, good night

was called, he said, by his American friends, "Hilary's relations." And there was a song which I only heard him

sing once; a passionate appeal to his friends to make a
place for him in Heaven. All I remember is:

> You with your teeth that hardly fit,
> And you with your idiot grin,
> Open wide those heavenly gates
> And let poor Hilary in.
> Poor old Hilary, dear old Hilary,
> Let poor Hilary in.

He had a very true voice for singing, a high tenor, which
was capable of tremendous power in the kind of song
which required roaring, and he was particularly fond of
the songs he had learnt in barrack rooms and on the
march. Whatever his mood, he would always sing anything anyone asked him to. At Rodmell, in spite of his constant telephoning, and the fact that he was always on his
way to some other place, he found contentment and ease.
I often used to think how he must have puzzled any
stranger who happened to be there, for in his choice of
songs he was as unpredictable to one who did not know
him as in everything else. Here you had what must surely
be a Frenchman singing a French song, but the next moment he might be singing with equal enjoyment a song of
the English music-halls or something from Pélissier's
"Follies," or some little lyric of his own, such as "The
Delicate Flower." He would switch from grave to gay, or
gay to grave, and, as I have said, the singing went on all
through meals. D. B. Wyndham Lewis told him once
when we were in Spain how wise he was to compose his
own music, and said: "Just imagine what some composer
would have made of the song about Miranda." And he
performed for us a highly amusing parody of any drawing-room ballad-melody, set to Belloc's words.

One day in the Temple Bar there was a rumour in the
air that J. B. Priestley was going to write a revue, and

would welcome contributions. When A. D. Peters was consulted about it, he was very guarded. Priestley himself was not there, but the rumour strengthened, and a dozen writers were discussing it, when Belloc arrived. I told him what the excitement was about, and he said: "He shall have one or two of my songs—but I shall insist on my own music to them. He must be told that he can't have them, unless they are sung to my tunes." For several days the rumour persisted. When Priestley came in, he was almost mobbed by his over-eager collaborators. When the noise had died down, he said he had no idea what on earth we were all talking about. He had no intention of writing a revue. And that was the end of that.

Apart from songs, Belloc had not much interest in music, and he could not stand piano-playing. He liked simple airs and uncomplicated melodies, voices not over-trained. Even without his French background, he would have detested Wagner. It was while he was a boy that the furious controversies about Wagner raged in Paris: with Déroulède and the Ligue des Patriotes (who saw the propaganda in the music) violently condemning it, and the world of the students and intellectuals equally violently praising it. Even Alphonse Daudet, who was on the side of the intellectuals, admitted that it was dangerous music, and as completely un-French as anything could be. I never heard of Belloc going to a concert, and I cannot imagine him having the patience to sit through one. Edmond Warre and I once went to "Cosi Fan Tutte" with him, and he seemed to enjoy it. Mozart was one of the composers whose music he liked, and his phrase "The Christian innocence of Mozart" is a good one. But it is odd that a man with such a true ear and such a gift for writing melodies for his own songs should not have been more interested in music. He came once to Rodmell with some verses which he had cut out of a paper. He had put them to a tune, and he sang them repeatedly; and I believe the tune to which we used to sing Hugo's "Guitare," the song of Gastibelza, was his own; as was, I hope, the tune of:

> Anne Boleyn had no breeches to wear,
> So the King got a sheepskin and cut her a pair;
> Skin side out and woolly side in—
> It was warm in the summer for Anne Boleyn.

❂   ❂   ❂   ❂   ❂

At Rodmell he talked a great deal about poetry, and was always speculating on the mystery of how great verse gets written; what it is that transmutes words into magic. For a great line of poetry is probably composed of words which we use every day. Yet when we read that line, it is as though we have come under a spell. He took as an instance of the magical quality in poetry the line

> And we in dreams behold the Hebrides.

If you write, "And we behold the Hebrides in dreams," you are back in this world again. The spell is broken. Why? You may say it is the order of the words, the rhythm, which casts the spell, but that is an unsatisfactory explanation. Belloc had no explanation of the mystery, and left it as something we cannot hope to understand on this side of the grave. The sonnet was bound to be a form which would attract him, because it is strictly disciplined. He said that it is the test of a poet, because a sonnet must be good all through, with no weak line to let it down, and make it sound like a cracked bell. "Anybody," he said, "who can write poetry can write a bad sonnet, or a sonnet with perhaps one or two good lines, but only a first-rate poet can write the fourteen good lines." As to his own poetry, he thought his small output of verse would be against its survival. When one considers the volume and variety of his other work, it is not surprising that he wrote so little poetry. But, apart from that, he laboured at it slowly, putting a poem away for years, then taking it out again; chiselling and polishing with the utmost care. In an essay called "The Unknown Country" he wrote:

> . . . Verse is a slow thing to create; nay, it is not really created: it is a secretion of the mind, it is a pearl that gathers round some irritant and slowly expresses the very essence of beauty and desire that has lain long, potential and unexpressed, in the mind of the man who secretes it.[1]

His poetry has its passionate admirers, but so far he has not been given the place to which he has a right as a poet. There are several obstacles in the way of his full recognition. I would not myself put small output amongst them. A. E. Housman's output was small. But his versatility is certainly an obstacle. So is the success of his widely quoted light verse. It is not customary for a man to be master of both comic and serious verse. Again, his poetry is in the tradition of English poetry. It is also intelligible and melodious, and not at all of the kind that is admired today. It is never what Mr. Ivor Brown has called "barbed-wire verse," which is so difficult to penetrate, and usually protects nothing but a refuse-heap. The present fashion will not last. Perhaps it will be succeeded by something even more debased. But, in the end, it is likely that men will demand food for the emotions once more, and will look for the music of poetry to uplift them. One may be thankful that Belloc was never tempted to re-write his early verse; a temptation to which Yeats yielded, with such deplorable results. Had Belloc been able to devote more time to poetry, we might have had that translation of the "Song of Roland" which he wanted to make. But he "Never in his rightful garden lingered." English poetry is the poorer, but we Catholics are the richer.

[1] *On Nothing, and Kindred Subjects.* (Dutton: 1925.)

3

DAYS AT SEA

ALL HIS LIFE BELLOC LOVED THE SEA. HE LOVED BOTH THE repose and the challenge. Many of his happiest days were spent sailing his own little boat, and some of his finest writing relates his adventures at sea, and the thoughts that came to him in storm and calm. There was recurrent in him a mood of rebellion against the cares of life and the incessant toil of writing to earn money. That mood is the theme of the "Stanzas written on Battersea Bridge during a South-Westerly Gale," and when I read the poem today I remembered how he would suddenly stand still in a London street, look up at the sky, gauge the wind, and say: "What a day for sailing! I wish we were aboard the *Nona*." The poem is also, like so many of his best essays, concerned with that last good landfall which no living man has seen, but which we all glimpse in our dreams. It is the vision of Hy Brasail, as one sees it from the western

edge of Ireland, but it is also a premonition. It is the haven
beyond Death which awaits those who have earned it.

He had sailed since early youth, and in later life took
every opportunity to set off on cruises of varying duration.
His two surviving sons, Hilary and Peter, inherited his
love of the sea, and it was by them that I was introduced
to the famous *Nona*. She was a nine-ton cutter, built somewhere about 1870 at Bembridge in the Isle of Wight, a
sturdy little boat made for leisurely fun, and not for rac-
ing. She was rather more than thirty feet over all, broad
in the beam, with a draught of five or six feet. My experience of boats had been confined to a boyhood holiday on
the Norfolk Broads, so that I was a mere cargo. Moreover
I have always been useless with my hands, clumsy to a
degree, and slow to understand technical matters. But my
apprenticeship was not a very serious affair. On one occasion we managed to get mixed up in a race at Cowes as we
were pottering about in those waters. We must have been
an odd sight among the beautifully painted yachts, with
their gleaming brass, and the owner, dressed up in nauti-
cal attire, spoke to us bluntly, as he would have spoken
to a stray dog. The stray dog snapped back at him, and we
lolloped clear of the race. On another occasion we left
Poole, and lay in the Hamble Mouth for the night. In
those days it was a serene and peaceful anchorage, and
we rowed ashore to a little inn, which I hope has survived
the coming of stink and noise to those parts.

Hilary Belloc went to America and Peter to Spain, and
it was only when the latter returned to England that I
again became a mariner. But there was an interlude. Belloc
had a second boat, an extraordinary sort of tub, which he
occasionally took out. It was said that when the wind blew
this strange craft moved sideways across the water. She
was, at this time, at Littlehampton, and one Sunday at
King's Land after Mass, Belloc said: "We'll go to Little-

hampton and bring the *Dreadnought*"—that was her proud name—"up river to Arundel. There's a man there who will look after her." So off to Littlehampton we went, found the *Dreadnought*, hoisted sail and set out to negotiate the tricky reaches and curves of the Arun. I tried to do what I was told, but somewhere near Ford we ran aground. We got overboard and endeavoured to push her clear, but she was firmly wedged in the mud, so we sat in a meadow and smoked, waiting for the tide to lift her off. Towards evening we grew tired of waiting. We set off across the fields, and went to Benediction in St. Philip Neri, and then to the hotel by the bridge in Arundel, after arranging with a man in the town to rescue the *Dreadnought*, and bring her up the river.

The Arun has been an unlucky river for me. On another occasion the two of us sailed the *Nona* up to Arundel. It was explained to me that our object was to moor her to a post below the bridge. Belloc would take the tiller. My task was to go forward when we drew near the place and to catch one of the posts with a boat-hook, hold on, and tie the rope securely round the post. It was a perfectly simple operation. The only thing to remember was that the current would be pretty swift and strong. If I made a mess of my job, the *Nona* would drift on, and anything might happen. Belloc was calm and businesslike as we came up the river, but the more he insisted on the importance of my part of the business, repeating clearly and precisely what I had to do, the more bothered I became. He was under no illusion as to my clumsiness, and he emphasized the simplicity of the plan. We came round a bend and got the sails down and stepped the mast, and my instructions were repeated. "Do you think you can do it?" he asked. "I can do it," I said grimly, and I went forward in plenty of time, clutching the boat-hook. The posts came into sight, and I chose one, and took up my position. I noticed how swiftly we were drifting on the tide. I gripped the hook, held myself tense, and, as we came abreast of the post I had chosen, struck fiercely. The hook caught the post, and I relaxed my effort, and made ready the rope in my other hand. The boat went on, the hook slipped, and I fell overboard into the Arun. The last words I heard from Belloc have become famous in both families. He shouted: "Are you drowning, my boy?" And I shouted back: "No. I'm all right." I was all right, but what of the *Nona?* By good fortune a man in a rowing boat arrested her course before she got to the bridge, and she was towed to a mooring. I scrambled out of the water, and rejoined my skipper in the hotel. We drank port, and he made no reference to my imbecility, but, standing in the window of the room where we were drinking, looked down at the river, and said, "I will now compare life to a river," which he did in a long passage of rhetoric.

To return to the *Dreadnought*. One day at Rodmell I received a telegram from Belloc, asking me to go to Newhaven, where she was then lying, and to tell the man who looked after her to have her ready to put to sea in a day or two. I don't know whither we were bound, but the boat had been neglected for a long time, and the cruise was abandoned. The man was accused of not doing his job, and the case was brought to Court at the Lewes Assizes. It became clear at the beginning of the hearing that the magnificent name *Dreadnought* had misled the Judge. He evidently saw her as an enormous yacht, with a trained crew to keep her spick and span, and ready to sail for Beaulieu or Cannes at a moment's notice. For he asked whether this one man was supposed to do all the work of maintenance and polishing, and so on, without any assistance. Anyhow, Belloc lost the case, and we spent a pleasant evening in the "White Hart." I never learned the ultimate end of the *Dreadnought,* but I never saw her again.

In 1926 Peter Belloc came back from Spain. The *Nona* was lying in one of the yards at Poole, in the charge of a man with a stiff neck, whom we called Col de Fer. In the summer it was decided that the three of us should set off on a cruise along the English coast, eastwards. At the beginning of July we came to Poole, laid in a stock of provisions, paraffin for the primus stove, and so on. I, not to be outdone as a sailor, bought, very cheap, an oilskin about four sizes too large for me, and a sou'wester—to the amusement of my companions. A commodore's hat for fine weather was suggested, and a smoking jacket for bridge-parties on deck. The little cabin of the *Nona,* in which there was not room to swing a novelist, had a narrow table, and a narrow bunk running along each side. Peter, being the youngest of us, was given as sleeping quarters the hole in which the anchor chain was coiled. And on this anchor chain he slept during the cruise, while we lolled at our ease on the bunks. On the eve of sailing we left Belloc on board, and made our last foray ashore. As a surprise for him and a pleasure for ourselves we bought a dozen bottles of non-descript Burgundy from the proprietor of a hotel whom we knew. These we smuggled aboard, while Belloc was busy with the charts. He knew the coast well, but he also knew that however experienced a sailor man may be, and however thorough his knowledge of any waters, there are always surprises, traps and other things incalculable. I remember my amazement when, on a former occasion, we had got stuck on a hidden sandbank outside this very harbour.

Next morning we sailed out of Poole Harbour, and rounded Hengestbury Head with a light following breeze. It was a bright morning, and we were all happy to be on our way. The *Nona* seemed to rejoice with us, and Peter and I took turns at the helm, while Belloc sang, told stories, and discussed the historical associations of the Dorset and Hampshire coasts. The weather grew duller and the breeze freshened as we came through the Solent, and presently a gloomy, drizzling rain began. That night we lay in Hamble Mouth. We sat up on deck in the darkness talking of this and that, after a meal of sardines and bread and biscuits in the little cabin, and we drank port from a big flask. Peter and I then sprang our surprise, to the delight of Belloc. But at the first sip there were groans and cries of mortification in chorus. The stuff was horrible, and anyone watching us drink would have thought we were taking some bitter medicine or other.

We were up early, and it was one of the rare days on which the primus stove was in reasonable working order. The plan for the day was to make for the Looe Stream, between Selsey Bill and the reef of rocks known as the Owers, and come through on the flood tide, and so sail eastwards along the Sussex coast. The weather was clear and there was just enough wind. But our progress was slow, and we missed the flood at the Looe, and had to stand out to sea, and get outside the Owers. The wind dropped, and a fog came down. There was nothing to do but wait. The *Nona* rolled and creaked and banged, and the fog thickened. We could see nothing. We had no outboard motor, as Belloc, rightly, objected to such mechanical contrivances. Belloc read Dickens in the cabin, and Peter and I talked on deck. The darkness came on, night fell, and there was not a breath of wind. Now and then we heard a fog-horn in the distance. All through the night we took it in turn to keep watch. I suppose it must have been some time after midnight when there was a sudden threshing sound, as though a huge sea was breaking, and a big ship passed within a few yards of us. She would have cut us in two had she hit us. For myself, I was terrified, but the other two took things as they came, and merely remarked that it was a lucky escape. In the morning the fog was still down, and the *Nona* was still rolling about impotently. But in the late afternoon a breath of wind thinned the fog. We felt life in the tiller, and at last were on the move again. The rags of fog wreathed away, and the lights of Worthing came up on our port bow. We were very tired, and decided to drop anchor off a breakwater. I was so pleased to see the dry land that I knew I was what Belloc called "a harbour chap," and that lying out to sea becalmed in a thick fog was not my *métier*.

We kept fairly close in-shore on the next day. There was a strong south-westerly wind, and one of those lumpy, following seas, under a heavy grey sky, which are a test for the helmsman. Belloc took the helm, and I set myself to learn how to dodge and outwit those great waves which come at you from all directions, any one of which may poop you. It was fascinating to see him glancing over his shoulder, preparing to meet the onslaught by a tug of the helm, and meeting it at exactly the right moment. It was a game of skill played against the blind force of the waves. The wind blew more and more strongly and the seas rose higher, but the boat was behaving nobly. Occasionally it seemed that one of the seething waves must flood over us— but it never happened. However, the weather became so bad that we decided to get into Newhaven Harbour, which we did. I remember the sudden coming into calmer water, and the loss of a feeling of exhilaration.

We dropped anchor, stowed sail, came ashore, and had a large meal at the inn where they say Louis Philippe began his exile in 1848. We spent the afternoon on board, and in the evening went to Rodmell to see the Allisons. They had guests, and everyone was in evening dress. Belloc had substituted a shirt and stiff collar for his seaman's jersey, and was presentable. Peter and I were unshaved, and dirty from head to foot, and a lady whom we had never met seemed to think we were the Something Trio from a circus. It was an embarrassing occasion, but the

Allisons were never at a loss, and the evening passed off happily enough for everyone. We returned to Newhaven and slept on board.

The strong winds and rough seas continued for the next two days. Looking back now, I cannot remember that we had any prepared meals. Everything aboard was hugger-mugger. The primus had overturned and rolled about the floor, and I remember that the biscuits tasted of paraffin, and there was a hole in the skylight where someone had put his foot through it. The portmanteau in which Belloc kept his shore-going shirt and tie and collar and a few other things had come in contact with some sardines. But it was all part of the fun, and those were memorable days. We had a bad time rounding Dungeness, and were glad to be lying at ease in Dover Harbour, and to go ashore for a full meal. Belloc at once bought all the papers he could lay his hands on, but he never lost the thread of a conversation, whatever he was doing. There, in Dover Harbour, the fog caught us again, but as soon as it had lifted we came out of our lair and more or less drifted past Folkestone and Sandgate.

We were off Hythe when the breeze freshened, and Belloc said: "Shall we go to France?" We agreed that was a good idea, so we put her about. The wind was just right for us, fresh enough, but not strong, and we made the crossing to Boulogne in 6½ hours (about thirty-one knots). It was an easy run, and I took the tiller for most of the time, having been given my course. It was a clear, sunny day, the little dancing waves sparkled, the *Nona* curvetted like a young horse, and we sang "In the days of Queen Victoria, they never did the things they do today," and the song which ends:

> What did Eve say to Adam,
> The saucy little madam?
> "Oh, Adam, you should eat more fruit."

We also sang French marching songs, and songs that Peter had brought back from Spain, and we were singing heartily when there appeared ahead of us what looked like a little race. We could see the broken water showing white, and all jumbled up and seething. It was the Colbart, a sandy reef to be avoided by the big ships; a little brother of the Varne, which is important enough to have a lightship. We went straight through the tumbling water and out the other side. When the bulk of Gris Nez came up out of the sea on our port bow, and we saw the bay of Ambleteuse, and Boulogne ahead of us, we began to talk of food and drink. We glided into the harbour, got down the sails and left the *Nona* to her repose, while we went ashore to dine like emperors at Mony's restaurant.

The next day we bought some provisions and wandered about the town. Then we took a train to Montreuil, and from there a car to the battlefield of Crécy. Belloc gave us a vivid description of the campaign preceding the battle, and of the battle itself, dropping now and then into French, as the astonished chauffeur was deeply interested. I remember wishing that history could be taught like this, for the battle came to life before our eyes. There were, of course, digressions dealing with the errors and the stupidities of the dons, and of historians who write of a battle without bothering to visit the site. He demonstrated how some of the accounts of the battle had got important points wrong. It was an excellent illustration of the method he used in his book *The Eye Witness*.

We went back to Boulogne, slept aboard, and the next day the weather was bad. There was a raging sea. "Shall we stay ashore, or put to sea?" asked Belloc. "Stay ashore," said I, "I'm a harbour chap in this sort of weather." "I thought we set out to do some sailing," said Peter, who was completely fearless. "What on earth is the point of hanging about on land, after coming as far as this?" Belloc seemed undecided, but, to my relief, supported me. He decided it was too stormy, and after some muttered remarks about a quiet game of tiddlywinks, Peter made the best of what to him was a bad job. We ate and drank plentifully, and wandered about the town, and I saw again Pont-de-Briques where Napoleon dictated the orders for the march that ended in Austerlitz, and where I started, in a cattle-waggon, for the trenches in 1915.

We sailed along the Ponthieu coast, intending to land at le Tréport for a while, as Belloc had a friend there. But we abandoned this idea and sailed on. We met occasional calms, and had to lie to, but during the night we got enough wind for our purpose. About midnight Belloc went below, and Peter and I stayed on deck. In the small hours of the morning we ran into sudden strong gusts, which are not uncommon off the Norman coast. As you approach Dieppe there are a number of narrow gullies down which the wind blows, and if you are close in-shore you get the full violence of them. Judging by the position of the Ailly light, the Phare d'Ailly which I had explored as a boy, we were somewhere off Berneval, where also I had spent happy summer days, when we caught a good buffeting. The *Nona* heeled over and "took it green." While we were thus scudding along, in what seemed to my amateur eyes imminent peril of capsizing, the sound of a cork popping came up the hatchway, and we heard Belloc shouting: "Without wine at sea, my children, we are as tinkling cymbals." Peter had the helm, but we were both so overcome with laughter that the boat was almost out of control. Noticing that something odd was going on, Belloc came on deck, told us we were fools, and set things right.

In the early morning we anchored in Dieppe Harbour, and lay on deck in the sun. We went ashore for lunch, which we had at the Arcades, an old favourite of Belloc's, and a restaurant I had known since boyhood. Peter and I left him to wander about France, and ourselves caught the night boat to Newhaven. We lay down on deck and slept the journey out.

     ❊   ❊   ❊   ❊   ❊

In the next year, 1927, I made my last appearance on the *Nona*. We sailed along the French coast, but, as in 1926, got becalmed in a fog. Edmund Warre, known far and wide as the Bear, was the fourth member of the crew, and he got into the dinghy and towed us into the nearest harbour, an amazing feat of strength and endurance for a man of fifty. The cruise we had anticipated became a land cruise. We went to Rouen, and to Lisieux, and ended up in Paris.

The *Nona* had begun to feel her age, and required doctoring and patching more and more frequently, and finally she died. You may read a great deal about her in Belloc's many books of essays and in *The Cruise of the "Nona."* Her death is described and her panegyric pronounced in the essay called "The Death of the Ship."[1] There her portrait is drawn ("Cod-fish nose and mackerel stern"), and her character described, with its idiosyncrasies and lovable flashes of temperament. Somewhere off the Norman coast she started a plank, dragged herself into harbour, and collapsed on the mud. "Very soon," says Belloc, "she with hammer and wedge was dissolved into her original elements—all that was mortal of her—and the rest is on the seas of Paradise. I wish I were there—already: now: at once: with her."

She was a heavy loss for her owner, and left him a store of mixed memories stretching over a long period of his life. He who was so restless and created such a tumult of energy about him on land became a different man at sea. His mind was refreshed and stimulated, and in all the happy

[1] *A Conversation with a Cat.* (Harper: 1931.)

interludes of sea-going he found relief from the anxieties
and labours of his daily life on land. He enjoyed to the
full the business of life on board, both the work for his
hands and his body, and the problems of wind and tide
and weather which have to be solved as you go along. To
sail with him was an education. His passion for history, for
seeing the past, was so strong that he had stored in his
mind some event of importance connected with almost
any stretch of coast-line, and he had the gift of making his
hearers see what he saw. How often I have heard him
point suddenly to an inlet or a hill or a flat plain, and tell its
story. Passing outside Rye, he would make you see it as it
was, and would explain how and when it dried out, and fit
it into the context of the surrounding country; and in the
English seas there was nearly always some personal adventure connected with a channel or a harbour or a head-
land. One such story told how he took on board a Welsh-
man who was loitering in some small port. It soon became
clear that the man knew little of the sea. After a run they
put into a sheltered anchorage, and at the right moment
Belloc shouted, "Let go the anchor!" Nothing happened.
"Let go the anchor!" Nothing happened. "Let go the anchor, man!" "I haf let go the anchor, but there wass no
chain attaaached."

❂   ❂   ❂   ❂   ❂

So many men mixed in Belloc that his variety was inexhaustible, and there could never be a dull moment. In
the flattest calm you were not bored, because he would
turn that or any other misadventure into a jest, and when
he grew weary of talking, he would sing. The "Chaunty of
the *Nona*" had not been composed at that time, but he
sang many of his own songs; also the ribaldries of the
French barrack rooms of his youth, and old music-hall
songs. Echoes of them come to me now, as I write, and I

see his blue eyes glinting with laughter, and hear the light tenor voice which came so surprisingly from a man of his build. There was an absurd song of two lines, sung to a melancholy tune:

> Si j'avais cent écus,
> J'achéterais un âne.

and another dirge:

> *Je voudrais mourir pour elle,*
> *Car, de toute la fête,*
> *Elle était la plus belle—*
> *Et la plus bête.*

and the roaring

> There was a steam-packet, a packet of fame,
> She was run by steam engines, the *Dreadnought* her name,
> So sing hey, little fishes, sing hey and sing ho,
> She's the packet for Dublin—Lord God, let her go!

and Gerald Griffin's "Eileen Aroon":

> . . . Castles are sacked in war,
> Chieftains are scattered far,
> Love is a guiding star,
> Eileen Aroon, Eileen Aroon;

and

> O father, dear father, come home to us now,
> For we want your old breeches to pawn,
> The cat has had kittens and run up the flue,
> And the row in the house has begun.
> Come ho-o-ome! Come ho-o-ome!
> Mother is waiting to welcome you in
> Behind the door with a rolling-pin—
> O fa-a-ather, dear fa-a-ather, come home!

There was "I'm not a glutton, but I do like pie," and the unprintable *"Y'avait un grenadier,"* with its eternal refrain:

Et zon, zon, zon, Lisette, ma Lisette,
Et zon, zon, zon, Lisette, ma Lison.

and "*La Jolie Paimpolaise*," and "*Les filles de Commercy*,"
and "*Si la Garonne avait voulu*," and Victor Hugo's song of
Gastibelza, "*Guitare*," and "*Les Montagnards*," and "The
Corn-Beef Can," and a thousand others.

As I look back I recall also those phrases of his which,
however familiar, never failed to amuse. I remember one
dark night when I was at the helm, and we had got off our
course. The sky was black with cloud, and I ought to have
picked up by now some light (I forget which) on my
starboard bow. Suddenly I heard Belloc's voice: "All we
ask," he said, "is a tall ship and a star to steer her by."
Sometimes, busy on deck, he would say: "We will now
drink, or perish miserably in the attempt." Or he would
say, in some moment of difficulty: "A few kind words
from the vicar of Lower Beeding, and all will be well."

I now print two letters Belloc wrote me in 1925, as they
are good examples of the care he took over details in his
"staff-work." They are two of very many letters of this
kind which are among my papers. The first begins without
any preliminary talk.

By motor first, and then train. I can manage to arrive at
Poole Station at 12.30 on Thursday next, the 27th, the train
coming from Wincanton at 11.34 and arriving therefore at
the up platform, as it goes on to Bournemouth. If you could
meet me at the train we would go on straight to Stiff-Neck
or Col-de-Fer and interview him strictly for the space of
one hour. Then lunch and take the 3 o'clock train back to
Southampton West, where George would meet us at 4. If
you are free, come on with me to King's Land that night in
the Ford, stopping to say howdydo to John Phillimore on
the way. Will you write to me here and confirm this? Or,
better still, wire, as the post takes sometimes just over a
day. The crab is: your train, leaving Waterloo at 8.30, gets

to Poole at 11.30, leaving one hour on your hands. But if in that interval you can see Stiff-Neck and arrange that he give us a full hour without delays on my arrival, that is time gained. Meanwhile you might write him a line saying we are coming. It is a mercy to find I can do the whole job in a day.

The second letter runs:

Do try and come sailing with me Friday next. It would mean the whole day away, from early morning till midnight, but you could be certain of getting back on Saturday morning early if you wanted to. I'll be in London on Tuesday, 1.30, and I'll come on to Shereff's by about a quarter to three, if you'd wait there—anyhow I'll get there before closing time, so wait for me, and if we miss, could you go to, or leave a message at the London Mercury? For if you and I miss at Shereff's—if, for instance I am too late, I shall go straight on to the London Mercury office.

Before the break-up of the *Nona*, I had become a land-lubber. Peter Belloc had married in the summer of 1927, and I in the autumn of the same year, and as I had always preferred walking to sailing, I spent my holidays on foot. There was another boat after the *Nona*, the *Jersey*, and Belloc never lost his love of sailing. Though, with increasing age, he could not be so active on board, he could always get a crew from among his friends.

I have said that what Belloc loved when he went sailing was both the repose and the challenge of the sea. It was at sea, when the conditions so allowed, that he came nearest to doing nothing. But it was also at sea that he had an opportunity for battle. In the course of his sailing life he had often been in peril of death, but the memory of those occasions never outweighed the pleasure he got from storms and hours of peril. He has described in detail an adventure in Bardsey Sound on the *Nona*, with half her canvas torn to rags and the helm out of control. He knew that death was probably to be the end of the matter, but he was startled at his own indifference.

> The sensation was as much like courage as lying in a hammock is like a hundred yards race. It had no relation to courage, or a right depreciation of this detestable little world, which can be so beautiful when it likes. . . . I had always particularly disliked the idea of death by drowning, and I had never believed a word of the stories which say that at the end it is a pleasant death. . . . But here in Bardsey Sound, I was indifferent, even to death by drowning. All I was really interested in was to watch what way we lost and what chance we had of getting through. Indeed, the whole question of fear is beyond analysis, and there is only one rule, which is, that a man must try to be so much master of himself that he shall be able to compel himself to do whatever is needful, fear or no fear. Whether there be merit or not in the absence of fear—which sentiment we commonly call courage when it is allied to action, may be, and has been discussed without conclusion, since men were men. The absence of fear makes an admirable show, and excites our respect in any man; but it is not dependent on the will. Here was I in very great peril indeed off Bardsey, and utterly careless whether the boat should sink or swim; yet was I the same man who, in a little freshness off the Owers a year or two ago, was as frightened as could well be —and with no cause. And if this be true of change of mood in one man, it must be true of the difference of mood in different men.[1]

He said once, when several of us were talking about courage and how it is admired, and when one man had said what a wonderful virtue it was: "Physical courage is not a virtue, it's a quality." For myself, I am contented to call it courage when a man who is afraid masters his fear, and forces himself to do what has to be done. That kind of courage he certainly had.

[1] *The Cruise of the "Nona."* (Houghton: 1925.)

Belloc kept certain social conventions when he went
ashore for a meal, or for a day in some port. The peaked
cap was discarded, and a bowler hat substituted for it; a
stiff shirt and collar were produced from the old portmanteau. He burnt red, not brown, and I never got used to the
flaming face under the bowler hat. As soon as he was
ashore, he would buy papers, and complain that, "all news
is now propaganda." He liked to get back to the boat as
soon as possible, because, when he touched dry land, his
worries and anxieties crowded about him, and there is
nothing more soothing to the mind than idling on deck, or
preparing for the next run. Nor is there anything more
restful than a quiet harbour, with evening coming on, and
the labours of the day finished. The riding light is lit, and
as night deepens and the stars come out, you are conscious
of those small sounds of lapping water which induce
contentment. Sometimes Belloc would lie on his bunk
reading a book, and on one such occasion it occurred to me
that it was a rare sight to see him so engaged. What he
read, he read very quickly, and he could get at the core of
a book by seeming merely to turn over the pages. Sometimes he would join us on deck and tell us about the
cruises of his youth with Philip Kershaw, and sometimes
the three of us would go below and sing songs. But what
I liked best was to lead him on to talk. It surprised me to
find how fond I had become of that little cabin of the
Nona. I can see it clearly today, and I can hear our chorus,
sung to an exceedingly dreary tune:

> Coom an' 'aave a tiddly at the FOU-OUNtain,
> Coom an' 'aave a tiddly at the FOU-OUNtain,
> Coom an' 'aave a tiddly at the FOU-OUNtain,
> Old man Tom stands treat.

4

IN LONDON

In the spring of 1924 i went to see peter belloc in Barcelona. He had come off the sea, and was working in the Plaza de Cataluña, in the offices of the Riegos y Fuerzas del Ebro. My cousin, Guy Morton, D. B. Wyndham Lewis and Henry Williamson met me in Bayonne. We went on to Pamplona, came back over Roncevaux under a full moon, and walked into St. Jean Pied-de-Port in the early morning. There was a brawl, in which the three took sides against me, because they wanted to sleep and I wanted to go on. Having insulted them grossly and called them milksops, I left them and went on by myself. I made my way to Oloron, up the Val d'Aspe, and over the Somport. Coming down by the Aragon to Jaca under the strong Spanish sun, I became sick and dizzy, and arrived in Jaca with a touch of the sun. A day in the hotel of Constancia Mur put me right and I went on by train to Barcelona. Peter Belloc was living in a little place in the hills above

Barcelona, Las Planas de Vallvidrera. After this I used to go out to see him there whenever I could get away. In the following year Bevan Wyndham Lewis and I went out together. We climbed into Andorra by a track which I have never found on any map—perhaps we made it up as we went along. We then came up the gorges of the Segre to Puigcerda, wandered about the Cerdagne, and so, by Ribas and Ripoll, to some place whose name I have forgotten. There we took a train to Barcelona. We had reckoned on meeting Peter, and going straight up to Vallvidrera, but we found his father with him, and we were all to meet Mervyn Herbert for dinner in Barcelona. We were filthy from head to foot, unshaved and maddened by hunger. Belloc took one look at us, and said: "Have you no ties you could put on?" We were disappointed that such a man should fuss about our clothes, but later on we realized how right he was to expect a rather more conventional appearance at dinner in a restaurant. We tried to clean and tidy ourselves in a hotel room, but we must have been a horrible sight.

After dinner, the four of us went up to Vallvidrera by the electric railway, and we hoped that Belloc would stay for some time. My memory of the next day is of the four of us trudging round Barcelona, while Peter made inquiries at all the shipping agencies for any kind of ship that would take his father to England—or to anywhere. There were intervals in which we sat in a shady square, or in a café on the Ramblas, and drank beer. In one such square there was a fountain playing, and the heat and dust and noise of Barcelona seemed very far away. Belloc loved such places, and spoke his contentment; and we three looked at each other hopefully, and cunningly ordered more drinks the moment his glass became empty. Perhaps, we thought, we could lull him to rest, and make him forget his purpose. But it was an idle dream. He was soon on his feet again, and, as far as I remember, he ended by taking a ticket for a train to somewhere in France, and the next morning he left.

He thoroughly enjoyed Vallvidrera. The small hotel was kept by a jovial Cuban named Zafon. There were only a few houses, and it was quiet and comparatively cool, and there was excellent Alella to drink. The wooded slopes above the plain of the Llobregat rose to the hill of Tibidabo, which could be reached by a path or by funicular. But here, as in the quiet square in Barcelona, Belloc was unable to "relax" for long. He was a wonderful companion, but we knew that he must always be on the move. Even when the railway ticket was bought, he had to plan ahead, arranging dates and stopping places. But we would all of us have given much to see him sit back, and to hear him say: "To the Devil with it all! I'll spend two or three days here doing nothing." A thing I never in my life heard him say.

On my visits to Barcelona Peter and I used to go deeper into Spain for a day or two, and then come back and wander in the Pyrenees. Wherever we went, to Segovia or Saragossa or Burgos or Toledo, and, of course, in the Pyrenees, Peter always had stories his father had told him of his adventures as a young man. We quarrelled frequently, as the closest friends always do under physical strain, and I can see him now across a table in a café in Pamplona on a dreary wet day; his eyes blazing, his face red with anger. "I'm sick and tired," he shouted, "of all this æsthetic nonsense of roaming about mountains." But I see him, also, in Auvergne, singing in the teeth of a bitter wind on the Col des Goules, on the road from Pontgibaud to Clermont-Ferrand (the road of his father's song "Auvergnat"). That was the day we drank in the house of old Mme. Dumas. I see him singing, again, under the Peña de Oroel during our advance on Tiermas, which he claimed to have surrounded and captured single-handed, while I was quarrelling with a red-eyed vagabond in a venta outside the place. And I see him singing, always singing, in that lonely inn of the Corrèze, where I fell in love at first sight with the shepherdess in the broad-brimmed hat. She crossed the threshold silently, and stood watching us, and spoke no word. But into the room with her came the old fairy tales and all the pastoral poetry of France. Our rough wine tasted like the Water of Youth. We sang for her, and she went out into the yard, and we saw her no more. Once more, I see us singing in turn to the fat hostess of Maussac, that good-tempered woman who listened with a beaming smile to a grave, operatic air:

> *Madame, O Madame!*
> *Partir, c'est mourir un peu.*
> *Qu'est-ce nous devons payer*
> *Tout ça?*
> *Madame, O Madame!*

He told her how he had walked up the valley of Cambras d'Aze and over the Noufonts pass, and how he had beaten the Abbot of Nuria at chess. And I told her how I had rushed the Bonaigua on a moonless night, and breakfasted on bear's flesh in Viella. The good dame held up her hands, threw back her head, and laughed, and laughed, and laughed, until it would have done your heart good to see her so happy. Far different was it with the shopkeeper who, on the French side of the bridge of Irun, was awakened in the early morning with the song about the woman with two heads.

❋   ❋   ❋   ❋   ❋

Belloc deplored the changes which were coming in the Pyrenean country, but he said, quite rightly, that, though places here and there might be ruined, there would always

remain, in that great area, enough unchanged country for
a man to lose the modern world. When I first knew the
Pyrenees they were building the railway that now runs
under the Somport to Jaca and Madrid. The tunnel, eight
kilometres long, had been made, but was only used by
workers crossing from Spain to France or France to Spain.
Once, when there was too much snow on the Somport, I
walked through this tunnel out of Spain, in the early morning, and got claustrophobia half-way through. There was,
of course, a railway up the Val d'Aspe from Oloron, but
it ended somewhere below Urdos. When, later on, I wrote
a book about the Pyrenees I described a night spent in a
little fonda at Forges d'Abel, and I received a letter saying that my description was very mystifying, as my correspondent could find nothing but an enormous international station, buffet and hotel. Returning to Luchon to
walk by the old track into the Val d'Aran, I found a motor-
road over the Portillon, and there is now a railway from
Foix up the Ariège valley and down into the Cerdague.
Today the railway runs all the way down the valley of
Canfranc, by the side of the noble river Aragon. I, and
many others, always assumed that the inn at Canfranc
was the inn of Miranda in the song "Tarantella." But
Belloc told me that he had no particular inn in mind when
he wrote the song.

   In a cave high in the mountains, near the source of the
Segre, Belloc once had a vivid dream, which he has told in
the essay "In Patria."[1] He had taken shelter at night in this
cave and had fallen asleep. Then it seemed to him that he
awoke, and saw the squat, misshapen figure of a little man
beckoning to him. He followed, and they came to the
crest of a ridge. As they waited side by side, the mist lifted,
and broad daylight revealed what was beneath them.

[1] *On Something.* (Dutton: 1931.)

Ten thousand feet below, at the foot of forest cascading into forest, stretched out into an endless day, was the Weald. There were the places I had always known, but not as I had known them: they were in another air. There was the ridge, and the river valley far off to the eastward, and Parham pines, Amberley Wild Brooks, and Petworth the little town, and I saw the Rough clearly, and the hills out beyond the county and beyond them farther plains, and all the fields and all the houses of the men I knew. Only it was much larger, and it was more intimate, and it was farther away, and it was certainly divine. A broad road such as we have not here and such as they have not in these hills, a road for armies, sank back and forth in great gradients down to the plain. These and the forests were foreign; the Weald below, so many thousand feet below, was not foreign but transformed. The dwarf went down that road. I did not follow him. I saw him clearly now. His curious little coat of mountain stuff, his thin, bent legs walking rapidly, and the chestnut sapling by which he walked, holding it in his hand by the middle. I could see the brown colour of it, and the shininess of the bark of it, and the ovals of white where the branchlings had been cut away. So I watched him as he went down and down the road. He never once looked back and he no longer beckoned me. In a moment, before a word could form in the mind, the mist had closed again and it was mortally cold; and with that cold there came to me an appalling knowledge that I was alone upon such a height and knew nothing of my way. The hand which I put to my shoulder where my blanket was found it wringing wet. The mist got greyer, my mind more confused as I struggled to re-member, and then I woke and found I was still in the cave. All that business had been a dream, but so vivid that I carried it all through the day, and carry it still.

This dream was only the poetry of those thoughts on

life and death which so constantly occupied his mind, and
sometimes broke into his conversation. Anybody familiar
with his work will recognize the theme. It recurs when he
is at sea or when some landscape seems to be a vision
rather than reality. It is the conviction that we exiles shall
one day find Beatitude, and that it will be like coming
home, because we shall see, transfigured, and never, never
more to be lost, all the common things of life which we
have loved so dearly. He recognized as a promise and a
reassurance that sudden movement of the heart which
answers the beauty of this world, and gives a meaning to
the mystery of our discontents.

He once said to me: "One of the bores of growing old
is that you lose your pleasure in landscape." But when I
first knew him he never could see the Downs as they
stand up when you come over the rise of ground by the
Crabtree Inn at Lower Beeding, or Bury Hill and the
Arundel gap from under Rackham Hill, without an excla-
mation of praise. He would point out the field where he
had sat reading Milton in his eighteenth year. All that part
of Sussex was the playground of his boyhood and early
manhood, and as he talked of it, one realized how strong
was his love of England. His sister Marie Belloc Lowndes
had found it much more difficult to adapt herself to English life in the village of Slindon.

There is a field near Balcombe where, as he told me, he
and Maurice Baring lay on the grass one summer day, and
bullied Chesterton into translating that great sonnet of
Du Bellay, "*Heureux qui comme Ulysse . . .*" The result
was one of the most successful translations of a poem in
our time. All over the county there were places with memories for him, but when he looked about him as he grew
older, he realized that the countryside he loved so deeply
was threatened, and he lived long enough to see what
he had dreaded. Many of the inns where he had drunk his

beer were being modernized, to suit the taste of a new generation. Woods were being destroyed, new roads were being made for the increasing motor-traffic, and the county, like so many other counties, was losing its character. Even the Downs were changing. But Shipley, still remote, consoled him.

Two things struck him about all these "developments" and "improvements." Everything was changing for the worse, never for the better. And there was no philosophy behind this busy destruction. It was something which simply happened—a kind of chaos. But he saw a certain good coming out of the increased movement of masses of people along main roads or by railways. These roads and railways canalized the traffic, with the result that people had no time for the by-roads and lanes. In the case of Sussex, the rush to the sea left the country in between the great roads neglected, and therefore without any immediate temptation to "develop." But that consoling thought took no account of airfields, dormitory towns and so on. As an example of what can be done to a beautiful countryside I would take Crawley and its surroundings. Belloc detested the clumsy transformation or disappearance of so much that he had known and loved, for the beauty of English landscape was a beauty found nowhere else, and whenever he came back from his travels, but especially if it was the springtime, he was intensely moved by that beauty, and saw it as something new, as a happy surprise. The woods and hills and fields inspired some of his best writing. A man who followed the journey of the "Four Men" would meet with many disappointments, but he would find certain things to reassure him—such as the Fountain Inn at Ashurst, and a few lonely stretches of the Downs.

     ❀   ❀   ❀   ❀   ❀

When the offices of the *London Mercury* were moved into Fleet Street there was a considerable migration to the Temple Bar, where Belloc often came. He and A. D. Peters and I lunched once or twice a week at the Gourmets in Lisle Street, and when Peter came back from Spain to go into journalism, he usually joined us. Belloc did a good deal of his work at these lunches. He would correct proofs, while carrying on a conversation and waiting for a telephone call. There was never any objection to the rest of us interrupting him, as he was always capable of dealing with half a dozen things simultaneously. Occasionally he would mutter: "What a life I lead!" If there was any delay in bringing wine or food, he would look at his watch and say: "We can't go on like this. It's intolerable." One day his first words were, as he sat down: "The fool Cromwell was always blubbering like a child, and throwing horse-dirt about, when he lost his temper." On another occasion he plunged, without prelude, into a parallel between the lives and achievements of Richelieu and Bismarck, a theme which he developed in a chapter of his *Richelieu*. When he talked on historical subjects, it was like a man thinking aloud, and the remarkable thing was that he was not getting his thoughts in order. They were already in order, and you could have taken down what he said and made an essay or an article of it, with very few changes. But even when he was full of some study which he was preparing, he always talked of a dozen other things with equal gusto and vivacity.

After lunch he would go off to the Reform Club or to Bell Yard to dictate, or to the London Library, but he nearly always planned to meet one of us or all of us for a drink before his dinner engagement—or, if there was no dinner engagement, we would dine together at Brice or the Escargot. He was fond of the Carlton Bar, and it was a frequent meeting place. At dinner he took things more easily; was in less of a hurry, and rarely corrected proofs. His old friend Edmond Warre often came to the Escargot. We would sit over our dinner, and then Belloc would go back to his room in Church Street, Kensington—what he called his *bouge*. As he slept badly, he was up early, heard Mass in the church next door, and then had coffee and bacon at some obscure eating-house. He would usually go to King's Land at the week-end, and whenever he could manage it he would go abroad for a few days.

I think it was in the Temple Bar that Belloc cut into a long and acrimonious discussion about kindness to animals. He said: "Kindness to animals means kindness to the animals you like, and too much fuss about it makes it a question of having nerves instead of principles." Who ever heard of anyone being kind to a cockroach? And it was there that he sang the song he had made up about the General Strike: "Rally round the rich, boys; up the millionaires!" When I say that he sang in the Temple Bar, I may be misunderstood. He was a man always careful of his dignity, and any idea of him publicly roaring a song in a London bar would be ludicrous. He sang quietly to the man he was talking to, or to a group of friends. For singing was natural to him. E. V. Lucas has left it on record that the first time he met him, he felt embarrassed, because Belloc sang all the way through lunch.

In the Temple Bar days, also, occurred the episode of the Drakenburg Society. Its origin is still mysterious—to me, anyhow, and I was a founder member, as it were. Squire was in touch with a Danish sea-captain who was anxious that due honour should be paid to a Danish sailor, Christian Drakenburg, who had died in Aarhus at the age of 146. A society was founded with this purpose, and the invitations went out for an inaugural lunch and meeting at the Cheshire Cheese, where the annual dinner of the Invalids Cricket Club was held. Most of the people

who came to the lunch had only the vaguest idea of what
the whole thing was about. Belloc arrived late, was called
on for a speech, and pretended to believe that the Drakenburg in question was the range of mountains in South
Africa, of which he said he knew nothing. He therefore
quoted Latin, and talked of other things, after briefly men-
tioning the mountains. At a subsequent lunch he made another speech deploring the premature death of the old
sailor. There were several dinners, attended by the Danish
captain, who had made up a song about his hero, which
we all learnt, and sang with great gusto. The Dane had an
enormous amount of literature printed, both prose and
poetry, and I used to receive packets of it by post from
Denmark. The Danish branch invited us to send members to Aarhus for a kind of Drakenburg festival, and we
sent two delegates, Hugh Mackintosh and another. They
were fêted for a week, and on their return it was carried
unanimously that they were now entitled to wear a green
fez. The society petered out after some years, but I continued to receive literature about the sailor for a long time,
right up to the second war.

Every year Squire's cricket team, the Invalids, had a
dinner at the Cheshire Cheese. I was not a member of
the team, but I went to most of the dinners. Belloc came
two or three times, and Chesterton, E. V. Lucas and E. C.
Bentley. "The Winged Horse" was always sung. The
speeches were few, and usually delivered to a sporadic ac-
companiment of song and insult. It was the time when
sea-shanties were very popular, and Hugh Mackintosh
and Peter Belloc had an inexhaustible supply of them, so
that nobody coming in, and hearing sea-songs, French
marching songs and Spanish songs would have guessed
that cricket was the occasion for the dinner. Bentley had
sat for the Brackenbury with Belloc, and he told me how
his hopes dwindled when he saw Belloc take one glance

at his paper, and begin to write, and go on writing without pause. Bentley's contribution to the singing was the first line of a song Belloc used to sing: *M. Charette a dit à ceux d'Ancenis*. . . . On one occasion, Belloc himself sang "The Winged Horse." Other favourites at the dinner were *"En passant par la Lorraine,"* "Next Gentleman, Please," "The Man who played the Oompah" (always sung by Squire), "Do you know the Sampan Man?", "Haul away, Joe," and a dirge-like song with the recurring line, "I want to be buried in Rutland, if there's room." Squire also used to sing "The Jolly Little Ogo-Pogo," and the interminable song about "Little Billee."

❀　　❀　　❀　　❀　　❀

When Peter Belloc came home from Spain, he joined me in the lodging house in Ebury Street where I had a room, but the manageress complained frequently of the noise, and we left for a house in Elizabeth Street, which we shared with Richard Viner and Cedric Ince. It was an extraordinary ménage. We had very little money between us, and when Richard Viner, who was our official spokesman, had to ask us for our share of the rent, there was always a row. I slept on the floor, and Peter on a broken truckle-bed in the same room. The other two had proper beds. We had an old car, purchased for £10, which went along with sudden leaps. It would bound forward, stop, and then bound forward again, with a rattling and shaking that knocked your teeth loose in your head. Belloc was highly delighted with this car, and when he was first introduced to it, stood on the pavement howling with laughter when we four announced that we were setting off for Rodmell. We got there in the small hours of the morning. In this London house there was always plenty of wine, and we even managed to entertain. I do not know how long we could have kept it up, but the adventure came to an end in

1927, the year in which both Peter and I were married. I still bear on my lower lip an honourable scar, to remind me of a brawl in that house of chaos.

Peter and Stella Benson were married in the Church of the Sacred Heart in Hove, and I was his best man. He and I spent the night before the marriage at the Royal Albion in Brighton, where there was a reception and a lunch the next day. A few months later came my own marriage, in Brompton Oratory. Belloc was there, with full and detailed advice about travel. Knowing that we were going to stop in Chester, on our way to Ireland, he said: "If you stay at such-and-such a hotel in Chester, avoid the bacon there like the plague. It is quite uneatable."

Within two years the Rodmell circle of friends had scattered. The Allisons moved to Itchenor, Shanks and the Clennell Wilkinsons and my wife and I to London. In 1929, at Lourdes, we heard of the death of Allison. Belloc had written, in his *Danton:* "When death suddenly strikes a friend, the picture which we carry of him in our minds is that of vigorous life. His last laughter, his last tones of health, his rapid step and his animated gesture reproduce his image for ever." Anyone can test the truth of that for himself. When I returned to Rodmell some years later, I found the village looking exactly as I remembered it, but it was not the same village. A light had gone out. All the way down the lane I half expected to see Allison coming towards me.

To Belloc this death was very bitter. He had lost so many of his dearest friends, and he was not a man who made new friends easily. Nor did he ever take part in the social life of literary men. He had, of course, friends in the literary world—Chesterton, Baring, MacCarthy—but he did not mix with large numbers of writers, as most writers do, either from policy, or because they enjoy being with those of their own trade. His interests were too varied, and the literary cocktail party had no attraction for him. The men and women of the world with whom he associated in London or in the country houses of the old families were more to his taste. He referred to them always as "the rich," and never hesitated to make fun of them to their faces, but he liked the cultured life of leisure which they were able to lead. He often said that he was completely out of place among them. He sometimes remarked, cynically enough, that the "rich" thought it smart and amusing to have a well-known writer in tow. But that was not how they looked at the matter. They valued his friendship, recognized greatness in him, and were most of them humble enough to be honoured by his presence.

For Maurice Baring, who belonged to both the literary and the aristocratic world, he had a very deep affection, and he talked a great deal of his slow and edifying death. When he praised he praised whole-heartedly, and he who read so little outside the reading necessary for his work was a strong admirer of Baring's novels. One of the things that appealed to him was Baring's restraint, his understatement, his hatred of excess—a remarkable quality in a novel nowadays. For myself, I believe *C* to be among the best novels of our time. Baring was one of the first men to recognize Belloc as an important poet. It was he who prophesied that the poems in the first small volume of 1896 would be read long after most of the contemporary poetry had been forgotten.

Belloc was utterly unlike any of his friends. He was on a different scale. Obviously he would stand out larger than life among ordinary people, but I always had the same feeling when I saw him with such men as Chesterton and Baring. And they, it was easy to realize, had the same feeling about him. They were no match for him. And that was due not only to his wide range of knowledge and his multiple interests, but also to the strength of his personality. His influence on Chesterton's thought (not on his style) was very considerable, and one can trace it in Chesterton's books. It was natural to couple two such outstanding writers together, and to imagine them as much the same sort of men. But no two men could have been more dissimilar, and I once heard Chesterton draw attention to this striking dissimilarity. He pictured his own nature as rambling and romantic. "I like gargoyles," he said, "and every kind of grotesque thing, whereas Belloc likes diagrams and military maps." He then developed his idea, showing how, in almost every respect, they differed from each other. But what is important is that about England and international affairs and the Church they usually agreed.

One night the three of us were in a taxi. Chesterton wanted to go to Artillery Mansions, where he lived when he was in London. "Where are you going?" asked Belloc. Chesterton told him. "Right," said Belloc, "I will drop you. But first I have one or two places to call at." He mentioned the places, and one of them was in Hampstead. Chesterton said that it would be simpler for him to get another cab and go home. "No, no," said Belloc, "I will drop you." Chesterton gave his high gurgling laugh, and said to me: "This is what Hilary[1] means by strategy." Finally we rolled round London in the cab. Now, if the positions had been reversed, Belloc would have still had his way. Chesterton couldn't be bothered to argue about it, and the rich absurdity of the arrangement appealed to his sense of humour. The story is some explanation of why many people contrasted the good-natured charm of Chesterton with a certain hardness in Belloc. That does not mean that Chesterton's will was weak and his ideas uncertain. It simply means that their natures were different. Chesterton was

[1] Belloc's friends called him Hilary, not Hilaire. Allison was the only one who called him Hilaire.

easy-going, Belloc was not. It was this difference in their natures which made Chesterton deplore what he called the "sundering quality" in Belloc's quarrels. When Belloc quarrelled it was no sham fight. It was battle, and he struck to kill, because, as he said, without battle there is no victory on this earth. This pugnacity of his friend, Chesterton admired immensely. He himself, who had had to lead a sedentary life, could respond with all his heart to the man of action, the rider of horses, the soldier, the sailor, the walker. "Belloc," he wrote in his Autobiography, "is an English poet, but a French soldier." And he took as an example of what the French military spirit had done for the English poet the revolutionary poem called "The Rebel." Chesterton pointed out that most revolutionary songs are militant, but, from a practical point of view, utterly vague and romantic. This poem, he said, has a plan of attack. It is a song of battle, with military details of how the battle is to be won. And it is full of hatred and violence.

On Belloc's sixtieth birthday, July 27th, 1930, he was given a dinner. Chesterton took the chair, and has left a description of the occasion. There was to be only one speech, made by the chairman when he presented the guest of honour with a drinking cup of gold. Belloc's reply was characteristic. Chesterton had praised his verse. Belloc said, wearily and rather sadly, that when he was young he had passionately wanted his verse to survive, but that, at sixty, he did not care very much what happened to it. Then, after a pause, he said: "I am told that at the age of seventy, a man begins to care again frightfully what happens to his verse. I hope I shall die at sixty-nine." He fired the last words like a shot, and sat down. Chesterton was then told by one of his neighbours that he ought to say a few words of thanks, on behalf of us all, to the organizer of the dinner. I forget who was named as the organizer, but the wrong man was thanked. He happened to be sitting on my right, and whether he genuinely believed it, or saw an easy way out, he rose and said that it was a mistake to thank him, as it was I, Morton, who had proposed the dinner and organized it. I was taken completely by surprise, and stood up to receive the applause. On my left was sitting A. D. Peters, whom I had every reason to believe to be responsible for the dinner. I therefore said that I could take no credit for the dinner, as I had had nothing to do with either suggesting it or arranging it. The whole thing was becoming ridiculous, so I added, as an afterthought, "as a matter of fact it was Peters who had given me the idea." What I had meant to say was that Peters was the man we should be thanking. Peters passed the ball to Squire, and Squire to Sir Alan Herbert. And then the whole thing did become ridiculous. Herbert, acting the part of a cockney town councillor or other official, complimented Duff Cooper on his idea of a dinner. Duff Cooper made a mock political speech, and so on, all round the room, until the forty or fifty men had all spoken. After which there were songs and talk.

❖   ❖   ❖   ❖   ❖

At this time Belloc looked much older than his sixty years. Overwork, lack of sleep, and no settled way of living were telling on him more and more. Yet in the years that followed he worked ever harder than before, pouring out novels and essays and articles and books of all kinds. But if we noticed any increased fatigue, it was only because of what he had been before. His vitality was still that of a man of forty, and, for all his complaints, was apparently inexhaustible. We continued to meet for lunch and dinner when he was in London, and in the Carlton Bar or Hennekey's in Holborn or the Bodega in Glasshouse Street. Peter, who was working in London, and "Bear"

Warre and A. D. Peters usually made up the party. He still went to sea whenever he could, with James Hall, an old and close friend of the family, W. N. Roughead, Dermot MacCarthy and Peter as the crew. Other members of the crew, at odd times, were A. D. Peters, Sir Alan Herbert and Lord Stanley of Alderley. Rodmell was gone, but there were a number of homes for him to visit, and his family were often at King's Land when he returned at the week-end.

My wife and I went down to King's Land one day for the great bottling ceremony. Belloc used to buy his table wine in France by the *barrique,* from Théophile Guillon of Nantes. The same man supplied him with a very sweet liqueur called Prieuré, of which he was fond. This liqueur was the successor at King's Land of a far nobler drink, the Izarra of the Basques, almost unknown outside the Basque country not so long ago, but now commercialized. For the bottling of the claret, a dry, clear day was chosen. The barrel was tapped. My wife, with a candle beside her, took the bottles from Peter and filled them, passing each full bottle to me, and I passed it to Belloc who sat with the corking machine. The whole art of the thing is to fill the bottle with unerring precision, so that there is just enough space between the base of the cork and the wine. The wine must not lap the base of the cork when the bottle is closed up. The comparative silence was broken at one point by Peter, who shouted to his father: "Was Browning a great poet, Papa?" And back came the answer: "No, my boy, a Jewish philosopher."

Belloc's approach to wine was what one would have expected, and what every sensible man's approach to wine is. He relied on his own taste, and drank what he liked, not what one is supposed to like. Taste being a matter for the individual, it is silly to argue about it. This is particularly so in dealing with ordinary wines, to be drunk every day.

Everybody who likes wine likes the great wines, unless he
has some defect in his palate. Their excellence is obvious,
and though six men will each express their appreciation in
different words, no one of them will call it a poor wine.
But with the smaller wines there is room for disagreement,
and one should always have the courage to follow one's
own taste. Nobody who has drunk wine all his life con-
demns little unimportant wines in the violent terms used
by those who have come comparatively late to wine-
drinking. If it be clean and sound, and as young as you
like, it will be better than some well-known wine badly
kept, served in a cradle, and probably either adulterated,
or having no relation to the label on the bottle. I am thankful that I began to drink wine when I was six. Each year
my father added less water to it. By the time I was nine
there was no water.

My old friend Maurice Healy made one of the most
startling discoveries of our time in the matter of wine. He
found on the wine list of a dining-car on the Great Western Railway a wine called Château Mille-Secousses! But
his researches revealed that there really was a Château
Mille-Secousses-Chenu-Lafitte, in Bourg. He wrote a rous-
ing song about his discovery, which is printed in his book,
Stay Me With Flagons.

Thanks to his retentive memory Belloc never forgot a
place where he had had good wine or good food, and
people who did not know him well sometimes thought he
was joking when he would tell them to go to some un-
heard-of little restaurant in a remote small town of France,
and to order such-and-such a wine. In the matter of food,
he was something of a puzzle. He ate, owing to his constant rushing about, at irregular hours, but was always
contented if he could get cold ham or bacon and eggs.
Sometimes he would carry bread and ham in his pocket
and produce it when he was hungry. For this purpose he

always carried a large clasp-knife, with a corkscrew attached. He came one night to the house of my brother-in-law, whose mother was staying with him, and who was not prepared for the highly unconventional habits of the guest. Belloc had, as usual, kept his cloak on, and during a conversation he hauled out of his pocket a piece of paper containing bread and ham. These he placed on a very handsome and valuable table by his side, and unclasping his knife, began to cut the ham. My brother-in-law's mother watched this performance with growing horror, and exchanged looks with her son, who tried to reassure her by signs, and to make her understand that there was nothing unusual going on. He would often come to our house in London in the evening and ask for a bottle of wine to go with whatever he had brought with him. Sometimes he was quite faint with hunger. At home he ate well, for he had succeeded in turning a local Sussex girl, who had nursed his children, into a first-class French cook. The meals were exquisitely prepared by her, and he could be sure of his favourite dishes—such as aubergines. In London restaurants he was not a big eater, and in the houses of his friends often asked for something simple that would not put anybody to much trouble. He never would touch mutton, and he never tired, in restaurants, of *moules marinières* and *raie au beurre noir*.

I spoke of his retentive memory. One day during the first war he was being driven along a French road by a young French staff officer. It was a cold evening, with snow on the ground. "Who," asked the officer, "is the best writer of prose in England today?" "I am," said Belloc. The officer considered this in silence. Presently he asked: "Who is your best living poet in England?" "I am," said Belloc. The young man, rather startled, made no comment. After a while Belloc said to him: "Are you fond of brandy?" "Certainly I am," said the officer, "especially on an evening like this." "Very well," said Belloc, "turn left off this road in a quarter of a mile or so. Go on for a mile, then turn right. We shall come to an inn of sorts, and there we will have some of the best brandy you ever tasted in your life." The officer followed instructions, they came to the inn, Belloc ordered the brandy, and the young man's eyes opened wide with astonishment, not unmixed with fear. "He thought I was some sort of magician," said Belloc when he told the story.

I find among my papers a letter he wrote to my wife in 1928, from Marlborough, and posted in Holyhead:

> . . . In Dijon do not fail to go to the 3 Pheasants restaurant. Order a steak to be grilled an hour before you eat, and a bottle of Richebourg 1919. It is (or was) the best wine I ever drank. Forbid them fiercely either to warm or decant it, which kills it. There is no proper place to sleep in Dijon, but good inns in the vineyard towns, such as Chambertin. The Hotel de la Cloche is vulgar, blasted expensive, and sham-good. I avoid it. I've just paid for a dozen of that brandy, and Johnny has paid me for ten bottles at 25/-each. He said he wanted them kept till his return. They will be at King's Land whenever you want them, either to fetch, or to be sent by rail. It is good stuff. I shall keep the odd two bottles.

It was in Dijon that I once heard a man crying the *Ami du Peuple*, Coty's paper, in the street. An old woman who was washing the steps of a house heard "*L'Ami du Peuple! L'Ami du Peuple!*" She looked up, and imitating the seller's voice, shouted "*Deux sous le kilo!*"

In another letter to my wife, written from Paris at the same period, while we were still in Rodmell, Belloc says:

> I had intended to write and thank you from Dieppe for your hospitality. I put it off till my head should cease to hurt me: as it has not ceased, and apparently never will, I write muddily today. Wyndham Lewis also is ill. He has a

frightful abscess on his jaw. Other news is that a friend of mine, an excellent Catholic, has done a bunk with another Catholic who has red hair. His wife, whom he thus abandons, is also a Catholic, and has red hair. He had already done a bunk some time ago with yet another Catholic lady with red hair. All this is perfectly true and only shows! It seems that red hair is nothing and Papistry insignificant, but the combination irresistible, except (I change my pen because the one I have hitherto been using is chaste and refuses to chronicle such things any further)—except, of course, in wives.

Other news is that the French have 144 million pounds over and above what they need, and that they propose to pay off part of the National Debt. And other news is that in England it's all the other way, and they propose to put on more taxation.

Other news is that it snows a blizzard, and that always gives me cold feet. Some say that my way to Vienna will be blocked, first in the Vosges, then in the Black Forest. They lie. No snow yet could impede my progress. Except once at Setif in Algiers when the drifts were out of Nature for size. When I went away from Rodmell I appreciated what a hellish shame it was for me to take your good room. If I had known what difficulty I was giving, I wouldn't have done it. Next time I come I will sleep in a chair or a shed rather than do such a thing all unconsciously again. But perhaps you will have left Rodmell. If you do, let me know. Why don't you and Johnny ever come to King's Land? You shall have the Blue Suite and the Persian sitting room as well, and a selection of the following wines and cordials:

Tawny port
Thick port
The very, very good brandy
The very good brandy
The good brandy
The rough brandy
Cherry brandy

Solera sherry
Madeira 80 years old, or rather 84, at least
Bristol Cream sherry
Lagune claret 1921
Larose claret 1923
Beaune 1923
Côtes de Beaune 1923
Saumur bubbly, any old year
Vermouth, real
Vermouth, chemical.

And your favourite Prieuré, or God's Cloy. I love it. The less you like it, the more for me, as the Emperor said of Mahommed the Magnificent's harem. I have forgotten a Nuits of '21, and a Chambertin of '19, also lots of Barsac and 800 bottles of vin ordinaire.

I must now stop, for my pen refuses again to write. I crossed in an oily calm. Twelve people on board, and one yellow man with knock knees and splay feet who played a loud gramophone all the way over in the smoking room.

❋   ❋   ❋   ❋   ❋

Sometimes we would meet for dinner and go on to a theatre. What Belloc enjoyed most was a music-hall, but there were few left, and those few were becoming Americanized, and the new kind of slick comedian was taking the place of the old popular figures. The wisecrack was superseding the joke. But I remember one turn which we always wanted to see again, and I wish I could recall the names of the two men, in order to praise them. There came on to the stage two small, dreamy looking, shabbily dressed men. They shuffled along, whispering to each other, and then took their stand, and began to perform the most astounding feats of strength with the utmost melancholy, and with an air of being bored to death by the whole business. Finally one stretched out his hand and lifted the other off the ground and high into the air and held him upside down above his head without any effort, using only one hand. Then the man in the air suddenly removed his hand from the grasp of his partner, and scratched his head, and you realized that wires were being used. They never spoke, but conversed in inaudible whispers, and appeared to be troubled and anxious all the time.

If Belloc was bored at the theatre, he showed his boredom, and bored or pleased, nothing could prevent him from expressing his opinion. Peter and I and our wives took him to see *The Immortal Hour*, and he was restless. On the entry of an old bearded Druid, he said with considerable vigour, and in his normal tone of voice, "Here comes old mossy-face again!" A rather larger party of us went to see a play the name of which I have forgotten. We had a box, and to reach it, had to disturb a number of people in the dress circle. We eventually settled ourselves and up went the curtain. A number of people began to talk broad cockney. "Oh, Lord!" said Belloc, "we can't go on like this. We must go, my children. I can't stand it. We must get away." So up we got, and disturbed the same line of people again. They perhaps thought this strange procession was part of the play—some interpolated jest. Anyhow we got clear, and went to, I think, the Alhambra. Arrived there, we all went into the bar. On emerging to go to our seats, we saw on the stage a horrible young man, who was whining a sentimental song. "Oh, Lord!" said Belloc, "this is abominable. We must get out." And out we went. The ladies in the party were laughing too much to be angry. "What is the world coming to?" asked Belloc.

His enthusiasms were generous and whole-hearted, and he took as much trouble to praise what he liked as to attack what he disliked. I persuaded him to go to the play called *Beggar on Horseback*, and he was so struck by it that he talked about it wherever he went, and wrote an essay about it in *The Saturday Review*. But he had a completely individual way of looking at things, and you never could be certain how a play would affect him. My wife and I and Mrs. Mervyn Herbert took him to a farce, with Leslie Henson in it. We found it highly amusing, but Belloc became more and more fidgety and depressed. His exclamations of astonishment every time we laughed made us laugh all the more. He simply could not understand why we found the situations and the dialogue funny. But he stuck it out manfully, and we never repeated that kind of experiment.

He and I went to a pantomime together, and for a long time he made no comment. But I knew what to expect. The silence was too unusual to last. Then on to the stage tripped a girl with a mass of long, golden hair, and began to sing. "She is Nordic," said Belloc, "and therefore possessed by devils." At a performance of *Twelfth Night* we sat in the dress circle. In front of us were a number of earnest-looking young women of the student type, with the short hair and shorn neck that was then the fashion. At the close of that lovely speech which begins, if I mistake not, "Build me a willow-cabin at your gates," Belloc said loudly: "Yes, I've felt all that myself, but I never could express it so well." The effect on the young women was worth going miles to see, and though I am ready to admit that he could be an embarrassing companion in a public place, it was the kind of companionship I enjoyed. There is too little of it in the world.

Sometimes things that embarrassed many of his friends were done with a purpose. He believed in "making a scene" if things went wrong in a restaurant, and I have yet to learn of a better way of getting what you want in a place where the service is bad. Most people prefer to suffer in silence; in what they imagine is dignified silence. Nothing can be more undignified than to allow the management of a place which makes you pay through the nose to play the fool with you. They at once despise you, and even the young waiters, infected by their elders, neglect you. Many of Belloc's friends used to dread the explosion, but it was very effective. One of the things that annoyed him—though this was not serious enough for a scene—was the delay in bringing the wine. He liked to have it on the table at the beginning of the meal. But in a place where he was not known, some waiter would often go through the business of chambrer-ing the bottle, which means in a restaurant, shoving it into hot water and murdering it. Chambrer means to put the wine in the room where it is to be drunk, some hours before the meal. There are differing opinions about the temperature at which a man likes to drink his wine, but nobody in his senses wants a suddenly heated bottle. Today I notice, now that the most ordinary doctored Médoc costs about fifteen shillings in a restaurant, the wine waiter will serve it in a basket, as though it were some rare vintage. The idea, I suppose, is that, as it costs you so much, you will like to have all the fiddle-faddle with it. However, the whole rhythm of modern life is against the drinking of wine. The young require something with a swift kick in it, and drink for excitement rather than enjoyment. They say that Foyot in Paris closed down because the proprietor saw an American shovelling sugar into a Cheval Blanc. I myself heard an American order a bottle of dry white wine in Grenoble, and tell his friend that it had gone sour. They called the waiter, who succeeded in making them understand that it was "dry" not "sour," and that what they wanted was a sweet white wine. So the change was made, and all was well.

The kind of people who say you must not make a scene are prepared to wait half an hour for a plate of tinned soup. They will also object to booing in the theatre, or to any strong protest anywhere—except when a dog is refused a seat in a train. Belloc, when he was with people who dreaded a row, tried very hard to be patient, but his suppressed anger made things much more uncomfortable for them than a brief outburst, which got things done. The insane closing hours were a constant source of annoyance to him, as they are to every normally constituted person. He used to laugh at the argument which runs: "The public houses are open for many hours, morning, evening and night. Surely those hours are long enough for people who want to go on drinking and drinking." That argument assumes that you want to drink the whole time the public houses are open. But you may be a man who wants one drink at 4.45 or at 11.30; and you can't get it. He always insisted that it is the brewers who must be cursed for the licensing hypocrisy.

My wife and I had dinner in Soho one night with Belloc and Sir Max Beerbohm. Beerbohm had been a friend of my father, and I first met him at Dieppe when I was a small boy. He was the complete dandy in those days, and I was quite overawed by the beauty of his clothes and the way he wore them. I had met him again at the house of Robert and Sylvia Lynd many years later. On the occasion of our dinner Belloc was at his most tempestuous, and Max Beerbohm sat chuckling quietly, and only occasionally putting in a word. He was enjoying himself thoroughly, and perhaps it occurred to him how skilfully he had caught the Belloc of that evening in his parody in *A Christmas Garland*. There was no telephoning to interrupt the meal, and as I looked at the two men it struck me that it was like being with a rather demure old uncle, who was secretly delighted with the tremendous gusto of his brilliant young nephew. There was a twinkle in his eye while he listened. When a lull came, for the ordering of food or wine, he talked to my wife. Then Belloc would be off again on a boiling flood of anecdote, wild exaggeration, startlingly controversial statement, hearty abuse of some public figure, and fantastic development of a hundred fanciful ideas. It was an astonishing performance, and as bracing as a great wind from the sea.

As an example of his domination of a large company, I recall an occasion when he and I dined with the late Duke of Westminster at his London house. The dinner began with general conversation, but as it went on it became obvious that everybody wanted to hear what Belloc was saying. All along the table heads craned forward and turned in his direction. He was, as always, completely unaware of this, and continued to talk without embarrassment. He was very fond of the Duke of Westminster, but as he said to me, had few opportunities of meeting him, because "One must not thrust oneself upon people of such great wealth. I wait until they approach me. The Pyrenees have got into his blood, and that is good for everyone." At this time there was some talk of the Duke starting *The Outlook* again, a weekly paper which he had owned. Belloc wrote to me: "I told him I would write for him, but not for pay."

Many people who have heard of Belloc's fame as a talker have an idea that those who associated with him were brow-beaten into listening, and were deprived of any power to contribute their own ideas by his overbearing manner; in other words, they were shouted down. This gives a wrong impression of him, as crudely blustering. A conceited man, aware of his gifts and talking for effect, and to show off, behaves in this manner. Belloc could be rude when he wanted to, but in nine cases out of ten people listened to him because they enjoyed listening to him. When he argued to make a point, he argued to convince by reasoning, and was as interested in anyone else's intelligent opposition as in his own presentation of a case. When he was merely talking copiously, because it was natural for him to talk copiously, he had no interest in his effect on his audience. He was talking out of a full mind and thoroughly enjoying himself. His manner was aggressive, and the accusation that he often monopolized the conversation is true, but only once did I hear this criticism made with any resentment. Usually people were quite contented to let him talk on. H. G. Wells once said to me, "Talking to Belloc is like trying to break into a hail-storm," but he said it with a sort of malicious amusement. The point I would make is that Belloc dominated not by insensitive loudness, but by the force of his character. He talked with authority, and his presence suggested authority. If some well-intentioned person, with nothing particular to say, but anxious to make a showing, broke into whatever Belloc was talking about, he was listened to with the utmost mildness, and I always noticed that if the remarks made were deplorably stupid, there would be no reply. Those who expected to see the unfortunate man crushed or ridiculed were disappointed. Belloc was incapable of the hypocrisy of pretending to agree with something he believed to be false, but his sensibility and courtesy forbade him to fight the unarmed.

5

DAYS OF TRAVEL

WHEN YOU TRAVELLED ABROAD WITH BELLOC YOU HAD, NOT one companion, but several; the historian, the poet, the soldier, and the man of wide culture who was passionately interested in architecture, in people, in food and drink.

Some may quarrel with the word "soldier," which I have used of him before. It may be objected that a short period of service in the French Artillery in time of peace hardly justifies the word soldier as applied to the ex-conscript in his late middle age. Nevertheless, I stick to the word. Belloc's temper was military.

His ability to read maps easily, his eye for country, his understanding of military strategy and tactics, his love of order and precision stamped him as a man who might well have been an admirable staff officer. It is, of course, still the fashion to repeat the old jibes about the articles which he wrote in *Land and Water* on the military operations of

the first war.[1] The silliest jibe was that he was proving over
and over again, by diagrams and statistics, that the Allies
were bound to win the war. He was certainly not foolish
enough to treat war as an affair of mathematics, whatever
indications could be drawn from casualty lists. A French
General had said to him when he was a youngster—and he
never forgot it—that war is *"une chose aléatoire,"* and his
own opinion, expressed in public, was that victory in war
is unpredictable, and that it is not the business of a military commentator, or of anyone else, to tell people that
victory is certain. You are dealing not only with material
things, but with human beings, and with their Creator.

He was supposed to be perpetually prophesying with
complete assurance—a thing quite alien to his nature when
he was dealing with war. What he did say was that other
things being equal, the victory in modern war goes usually
to the side which has superiority of numbers and material. Battles, said Foch, are won in the soul, and the soul
is one of the "other things."

In the fourth of her four volumes of autobiography
Mrs. Belloc Lowndes tells of an occasion when he based a
forecast on a purely mathematical calculation. She was
staying with Lady Jekyll in December 1915. Lord Hal-
dane, Lady Horner and Belloc were among the other
guests. Belloc told them, in considerable detail, and with
surprising assurance, what was going to happen in the
Balkans, and he said there would be a withdrawal to Sa-
lonika. All those present, including his sister, disagreed
with him. Someone asked him why he felt so certain that
he was right, and he said that his prediction was a mathematical certainty. Without Russian or Italian help, the
Allies would be outnumbered by five to one. "Within a
month everything he foretold did actually take place."

[1] He had wanted to join the Army, and would have been invaluable as
a liaison officer, but, as he once told me, "They wouldn't have me."

The accusation that Belloc's deductions from figures were an attempt to make everything look rosy, because, like some patriotic Boy Scout, he felt constrained to preach the duty of cheerfulness, is too contemptible to be discussed. I will end this digression by asserting that nobody who is familiar with his descriptions of battles and with his other writings upon military matters could either doubt his ability in this department of literature, or believe that he thought warfare could be reduced to a mathematical formula. In *A General Sketch of the European War: First Phase*, he writes of his figures for the opposing strengths of the armies: "It will almost certainly be found, when full details are available after the war, that the most careful estimates have been grievously erroneous in some particular. Almost every statement of fact in this department can be reasonably challenged, and the evidence upon matters which in civilian life are amply recorded and easily ascertainable, is, in this department, everywhere purposely confused and falsified."

✿   ✿   ✿   ✿   ✿

Belloc's visual imagination was so powerful that he made you see the past. When he came to a town he knew its history, and would at once begin to talk about what had happened there, why the town had grown up in that particular spot, why it had or had not decayed. He would say, "The whole point of the place, its whole meaning is . . ." and then pour out facts and theories and suppositions for as long as you cared to listen. He was never contented until he had found a solution to some problem in connexion with the place. Why was there no bridge up-stream above such-and-such a village? Why was the attack made on the best-defended side of the place? How did they get guns through the marshes? Why did the population suddenly diminish at a certain period? He was never contented to read about anything—he always wanted to see it with his own eyes, to stand on the spot where great decisions had been made and call up round him the actors in some historical event. And, for this reason, he would go to endless trouble to uncover the past from beneath the buildings and streets of the present. Then again, he liked to stand in front of some ancient cathedral and talk of the various influences which had mixed or succeeded each other; to catch some feature in which a new style of architecture began to merge with the old.

He always insisted on approaching a place so as to get the best of it, to savour it. Chartres had to be entered by the Porte Guillaume, with the Cathedral standing right up above you. If you arrive by train, and walk into the town from the station, as I had done until he showed me the advantage of his way, you lose a valuable experience. Chinon I had always approached from the north, and, of course, missed the great sight of the ruins of the castle on its hill which you get by coming in from the south, over the bridge from the Faubourg St. Jacques. Then you see not only the enormous ruins, but the delightful little town itself beneath them, and the embankment where the old rampart used to be. We came to Chinon from Saumur, by little Montsoreau, where the Vienne flows into the Loire, and had the view of the castle across the water on a clear day of summer.

We came to Chartres across the Beauce, and in by the Porte Guillaume, and we spent a long time looking at those matchless carvings in the ambulatory, illustrating the life of Our Lady. When we came out Belloc was very quiet, and then I heard him say, not addressing me, but speaking a thought to himself: "Only the hands can make what the soul has felt." We found a very small restaurant where the proprietor roasted for us a chicken on the spit, and we talked about Marceau, whose statue is nearby, and about Fleurus, and about the overture to Fleurus and the great year of victory, Tourcoing, on which Belloc wrote a book in his series of six British battles. Next day we went on to the Perche country, and during lunch in a little town we saw the smallest pickpocket in Europe. He was a tiny child about a foot high, and he crept out of some passage and into the room where we were having lunch. We saw a movement among the overcoats on the pegs at the end of the room, and then a hand went into a pocket. Some sound disturbed him, and he toddled away into the passage. We wondered whether he was a free lance, or had been trained by the proprietor, and put on the staff. Back in England Belloc began a conversation one day by saying: "In the Perche they teach the children to become pickpockets from their tenderest years." "How's that," somebody said, "for one of Belloc's wild, sweeping statements?" "But," said I, "it is true. There is a Guild of Infant Pickpockets." After that it became common to hear one of us say: "In the Perche, where all the children are pickpockets . . ." It reminded me of Belloc's reply to an American journalist who asked him a question about English railway porters: "They all have blue eyes, and their golden hair is hanging down their backs."

Belloc's idiosyncrasies were well known to his friends, and one came to enjoy them instead of being irritated by them. Being a bad sleeper, he liked to get up very early and to be on the move. He always struck me as being indifferent to heat or cold, and to be able to go without food for long periods without any inconvenience. Often we set off without breaking our fast—a thing I found most unpleasant. One needed to be strong and healthy to travel with him, and to be ready for discomfort and unceasing movement. He always carried the *Indicateur Chaix* and many maps, and he liked to make the most elaborate plans. He would say: "Now when we get to A, we shall have time for a drink. Then we go to the Square and get the 'bus which will probably miss the train at B. We then walk to C, and get there just in time for the little tram-train that goes to D." If he made an error in his planning, he always laughed at himself. Once in Brittany we were following a route which he had spent a long time in working out. We suddenly realized we were on the wrong train, and all the arrangements had fallen to pieces. He was not in the least disturbed, but pulled out the *Chaix* and a map, and started to make a fresh plan. By train, 'bus, tram, hired car, with interludes on foot, a large amount of ground was covered, and I certainly learned more in that way than in more leisurely travel with anyone else.

Allison used to get a great fun out of all this planning in England, but had an idea that things would be different abroad. When he and I were to meet Belloc in Brussels, he said: "I look forward to this. We'll have a long evening in Brussels, and a great meal at our ease." "Expect no such thing," said I. "He will be on the platform to meet us, portmanteau in hand, and he will say, 'My children, we have very little time.'"

When we got to Brussels, there was Belloc on the platform, bag in hand, and his first words were, "My children, we have very little time." There was a hasty meal, and then we went off to Namur. The Hôtel d'Harscamp had changed management, and it was touch and go whether we should stay there, or go on somewhere else. In the end, we stayed there, and went on next day down the gorges of the Meuse to Rethel. One night at dinner Belloc was working out the next day's journey. Allison watched him with a quiet amusement. When the work was completed, and Belloc had explained how everything was dovetailed and our stopping places arranged, with a particularly compli-cated end to the day when, "We shall just have time to run across the Square from the 'bus to the station," Allison said, "Well, you can forget all that. I've hired a car." "Just as you like," said Belloc, and we heard no more of that plan.

Belloc was always happiest when he found some hotel or restaurant, known for many years—perhaps since his early youth—which had not changed. For "everything," he always said, "changes for the worse." He would never, if he could help it, go near the huge modern hotels or restaurants. In Brussels the Ecrevisse was his favourite eating-house, but last time I looked for it, it had gone. In Amiens there was a place to which he had first come as a young artilleryman. We went there together, and an elderly woman served us. "She was a little girl when I first came here," he said. The Lion d'Or at Perpignan, another favourite of his, was still as hard to find when I was last in the town, and the hotel of Constancia Mur in Jaca looked like remaining its modest self for ever. His objection to the big modern places was the incessant noise, the bare-faced robbery, the bad food, and the company.

❖   ❖   ❖   ❖   ❖

The first time I went abroad with him we took an American line from Southampton, which was calling at Cherbourg. There was music at lunch, so we left the dining-room hurriedly. Being new to the game of travelling with him abroad, I had not reckoned on irregular meals, and had brought nothing to sustain me. We were kept on board till late at night, waiting for a tender to take us ashore, and it was about ten o'clock before we got our next meal. We then went, by the first train in the morning, to Coutances and Avranches, and I remember, on the next day, stumbling down a hillside in the darkness before dawn to catch a train. We had no breakfast. We spent the morning exploring Mont St. Michel, and I was so weak with hunger that I had to drag him away to Mother Poulard. I have a later memory of running to the station in the dawn at Chinon, and of hearing his voice behind me: "You carry my bag. You're younger than I am." To get a picture of him on such occasions, one must see a square-shouldered, thick-set figure, dressed in black broadcloth, black hat, black tie and stiff collar. He carries a very old portmanteau. His pockets are stuffed with papers. He moves rapidly, with an aggressive half run, half walk, his feet shuffling along the ground. He will be cursing as he goes along, but in the merriest fashion; or, possibly, making fun of us both for "Going on like this."

"Bear" Warre, Peter, he and I were once walking (against time, of course) through a Norman forest. All the while he kept up such a running fire of high-spirited grumbling, with sudden invective against the whole lot of us, that we were exhausted with laughter. Then, without warning, he began to talk about the evolution of the wheel, and we were listening interestedly when the cursing began again, much louder, much more violent. We three rolled about, and the din was terrific. Anyone meeting us would have taken us for a party of lunatics. But we met nobody, and in the boiling hot weather we blundered on through the forest, howling with laughter.

His plans, though made with such care and worked out in such minute detail, were never allowed to interfere with a sudden impulse. For his curiosity was inexhaustible for new places; and when a place was not new to him, he liked to share his knowledge of it with you. As it says in "The Death of Wandering Peter":

> Look you, good people all, in your little passage through the daylight, get to see as many hills and buildings and rivers, fields, books, men, horses, ships and precious stones as you can possibly manage to do. Or else stay in one village and marry in it and die there. For one of these two fates is the best fate for every man. Either to be what I have been,

a wanderer with all the bitterness of it, or to stay at home
and hear in one's garden the voice of God.[1]

Sometimes there would come over him a mood of quiet
and melancholy, generally in some little place where he
could hear an early Mass and then sit in a café, reading the
paper, or writing to a friend at home. One such place we
went to together, and to which he returned whenever he
could, was Clères in Normandy. There was a simple little
inn, with everything decent and orderly and made for repose. We were the only travellers there, and in the morning we went to Mass, and then had our coffee and rolls in
such a leisurely way that I half expected Belloc to stay
there for a few days. But he could not be still for long. At
St. Valéry-sur-Somme, another village as careless of time
as an Irish village, it was the same. In such places he would
talk about his experiences of life. Once in a little French
town he said suddenly: "I would like to stay here and
write a book about life and death." What a book it would
have been, if he could have put aside all his other work,
and his cares and troubles, and remained there; and if he
could have borne to be alone for long enough. We should
have had, also, more poetry from him. More than once he
said to me: "I'd like to finish my 'Dream of a Conscript of
'92' before I die, and also my 'Ode to the West Wind.'"
Luckily he finished his poem on wine, on which he was
working for so many years. It was by his poetry that he
wanted to be remembered, and in one of his best-known
poems he writes:

> England, to me that never have malingered,
>   Nor spoken falsely, nor your flattery used,
> Nor even in my rightful garden lingered:—
>   What have you not refused?

[1] *On Something.* (Dutton: 1931.)

Some have thought his rightful garden meant France. But he told F. J. Sheed that it meant that he had abandoned poetry for prose, "because one fights with prose."

Sometimes, when the melancholy mood was over him, he allowed you to see deep into his mind. Usually it was a mere flash; a phrase which escaped him. But he had too much courage and too much dignity to allow a mood of depression to last long, and his boisterous form of grumbling never embarrassed anyone. On the contrary, one would have missed it. It was part of his character. While travelling he was nearly always in good spirits, and as he saw every landscape in its historical context, he was a most invigorating companion.

I say that he would never allow his plans to interfere with an impulse, while travelling. We were one day going along the road that runs from Châlons-sur-Marne, where we had been staying at the hotel with the magnificent name, the Haute-Mère-Dieu, to Suippes. Belloc pointed out the distant marshes of St. Gond, and talked of the Battle of the Marne, and of Foch's switch of the 42nd Division under Grossetti from the left to the right in the middle of the battle. He had, by the way, in a little frame, a sketch which Foch made for him of this operation. Suddenly he said: "Now I'll show you an extraordinary thing." He told the driver of our car to turn down a by-road leading to a little hamlet called La Cheppe. Before we got to this little place, he stopped the driver, and we got out. We crossed a streamlet, and came to a great circular fortification of grass mounds. Round us spread the plains of the Marne, the Catalaunian Fields. South-eastwards were the St. Gond marshes, north-eastwards the wooded heights of the Argonne, and beneath them Valmy and Ste. Menehould; every inch of the vast area soaked in history. And these earthworks were the Camp d'Attila, the fortified camp in which the Hun made his last stand. This was the place to which he fell back before the armies of Ætius and Theodoric. Here, fifteen hundred years ago, in the centre of the camp, Attila built the vast pyre on which he swore to perish rather than fall into the enemy's hands. But the attack was not pressed home, he was able to retreat across the Rhine, and returned to his own lands. It was an astonishing sight. We could even see the openings in the grass rampart through which the Huns came for water. Over the place hung that silence of old battlefields, which is not an absence of sound, but rather a haunting memory in the air, a still active memory. Next day, we went to see how the restoration of Rheims Cathedral was going on.

If my memory serves me, Falaise once held us for two days and nights. We looked out of a window in the castle, and below us was a stream, with a woman washing clothes in it, and in the air, the unmistakable smell of a tannery. We did not ask whether the woman was the tanner's daughter. Perhaps her name was Arlette, and we had got mixed up in the space-time continuum theory. Falaise has one of those violent equestrian statues which I like so much; William on his horse, charging, and another such statue is the St. Joan at Chinon. We went on to Le Mans, where there is, or was, a delightful restaurant by the bridge over the Huisne. It was a warm day, and we had our lunch in the shady garden, before making for the Perche country. I think it was about this time that the sundial game was invented by Belloc. We each made up suitable, or unsuitable, rhymes for a sundial. In Belloc's collected verse will be found one or two of the epigrams composed while it was still a game, and also some examples of what happened when the game became a serious exercise. I think the best of Belloc's sundial epigrams is:

> Here in a lonely glade forgotten, I
> Mark the tremendous process of the sky.

So does your inmost soul, forgotten, mark
The Dawn, the Noon, the coming of the Dark.

Or, perhaps:

Stealthy the silent hours advance, and still;
And each may wound you,—and the last shall kill.

*   *   *   *   *

One took Belloc's amazing physique for granted, but
even when he was unwell he never bothered about himself.
I had only one experience in all the times I was abroad
with him of what, in anyone else, might have been a
collapse. We were wandering about near Paris, and had
been to Montfort l'Amaury, to see the ruins of the castle
which was the cradle of the great family of Montfort. At
Rambouillet, Belloc began to lose his voice, and to feel unwell. Of course he would do nothing about it. He always
said: "People can only get patched up when they reach a
certain age. It doesn't do any good." We went back to
Paris, to the Beaujolais, which looks out on to the Palais
Royal Gardens, and he became feverish. He lost his appetite, and could only talk in a hoarse voice, but he would not
rest or go to a doctor. We spent an evening with French
friends, and I became anxious about him. Next day he was
worse. He obviously had a pretty high temperature, and
could only talk in a whisper. No meals are served in the
Beaujolais, so we had to go out, and he drank some coffee.
I implored him to go to bed, but it was no use. He had written to some other French friends, and was determined to
see them, so I rang them up and made the engagement for
lunch on that day. We went to lunch, and I never saw a
more amazing performance. He entertained the roomful,
talking, in that hoarse whisper, on anything and everything. He carried the whole party on his shoulders. When
it was over we went back to the hotel, and I induced him
to go to bed. He lay down for a couple of hours, and then

got up again, and seemed to be rather better. We walked about, and finally we went and sat in the Source on the boulevard St. Michel. He drank some beer, but had no appetite for his dinner. Next day, we came back to England, and for a week or two he was still unwell. I imagine he had quinsy, but he certainly did not care twopence, and relied on his stamina to keep him going; which it did.

Every street in Paris had either an historical or a personal memory for him. He detested all the racket of the traffic, but knew where to go for comparative quiet. He was very fond of a little restaurant called the Vendanges de Bourgogne, and of the Closerie des Lilas, once a *guinguette* on the Orleans road, and a famous rendezvous of poets in our own time, with Rude's statue of Ney close by, near the place where he was shot. What surprised me was that in Paris Belloc did not talk much of his boyhood, for he used to return with his mother every year to La Celle, the village where he was born. I did not like to suggest going there with him, as I knew too well the Sailor's reasons, in the *Four Men*, for not going back to the inn at Bramber. It was only later that I went there alone, and climbed to the little hill-top cemetery where his grandmother, his father and Mlle. de Montgolfier are buried, and Paul Déroulède. I saw, leaning against Déroulède's grave, the old German frontier post, marked "Deutsches Reich," which the French troops sent to Paris when they swept over the Vosges in August 1914. The Déroulèdes were friends of the Belloc family, and lived three miles away at Croissy. I remember once standing in front of a large picture, crowded with figures, at Versailles. Several people came up to look at it, and an elderly man said repeatedly to anyone who would listen, and in a voice made of all the elegies of the world: "That's Déroulède—that one there. That's Déroulède. That's Déroulède. That's Déroulède."

Paris, of course, always stirred Belloc's imagination. In

spite of modern developments he was aware of the bones
of the past underneath every quarter of the city, and for
his book *Paris*[1] he made the most careful and extensive
researches, and devoted half the book to the origins, "because in history we ought not to look down a perspective,
but to travel along a road." In the Preface which he wrote
for his *Robespierre*[2] he put very clearly the influence upon
him of the past in such a city—particularly the memories
of the Revolution which were in his blood. He tells how
he would sit alone in a room near the rue St. Honoré, hearing "the rumble of the guns, and the high palaces of the
city full of the people conquering." The great figures came
before him in his solitude: Danton, Saint-Just, Carnot,
Vergniaud. "Had such a dreaming reposed upon mere
fancies, it would have been proper food for poetry or for
fiction, but the deeds of the men whose story proved so
great that it could thus rise from the dead, were true. The
lives had been lived and the things done. Then it was not
possible to rest content in the shadows; it became necessary to fill out the whole truth, and since one was already
certain of the idea in which all these things were con-
tained, it became a business to explore their reality. For
this there was no refuge but history." The result of these
reveries we have in the three great books: *Danton, Robespierre* and *Marie-Antoinette*.

When he talked of such matters, he made the story come
alive, and you felt that when he looked at the site of some
building now gone, even that building rose from the dead
and was before his eyes; that the scenes in which his mind
was busy were present to him, and more vivid than what
actually surrounded him.

In Paris, and, in fact, in any place where the noise was

[1] Methuen: 1900.
[2] Nisbet: 1901.

overpowering, he always expressed amazement that most people do not seem to notice noise. It does not jangle our nerves, because it is now the background to all our lives. In the days when we travelled together, the wireless had not become universal, nor was it the custom, as it is now, to turn it on and leave it on, so that an unceasing slime of sound comes oozing into the atmosphere. Nobody listens, but nobody seems to mind. He loathed, also, a strident orchestra in a café or during a meal. If there was to be music, let it be distant and quiet. I remember an instance of the folly of returning to a place and expecting, nowadays, to find it unchanged. There was a Norman inn beloved of my father. He and my mother and I used to drive to it in a carriage when I was a small boy. A little clear stream ran through the garden, and one evening a woman standing by this stream began to sing. Her voice was the most beautiful sound I had ever heard, and the song she sang was the heart-rending song of Florian, Marie-Antoinette's *Plaisir d'Amour.* It was an experience I have never forgotten, and I suppose it was the song in the dusk that made me keep an idealized picture of the inn and the garden. Anyhow, happening to be in Rouen one day, I spoke of this inn, and we went to see it. It was like a madhouse. The road outside was blocked with charabancs and cars, and the garden swarmed with yelling crowds, and my picture of it was gashed and smudged and destroyed in an instant.

While walking in Normandy we discovered, in a little valley, a village so full of peace, that I will not mention its name, in case it has, by some miracle, survived. The road led nowhere in particular. We had set out on foot early in the morning, and I well remember the walk because Belloc was explaining the campaign of Edward III before Crécy; the advance from the Cotentin to Poissy, the retreat, and the fording of the Somme at Blanchetaque. As always, he assumed that his hearer had a detailed knowledge of the subject, and by the time he had finished I could certainly have written an essay on it. He had, as we may learn from his book on Crécy, gone over the ground with the utmost care, especially in the matter of the fording of the river. One has plenty of opportunities of reading about campaigns, or of hearing lectures on them, but I have never felt that the author or the lecturer, though he may have studied all the documents, had gone to look at the thing with his own eyes, had walked over the ground and puzzled out the problems on the spot; or that he had bothered about tides or meteorological conditions. Here is a specimen footnote to Belloc's Crécy, referring to the crossing of the ford: *The low tide after the full moon occurs on August 24th at about half-past six o'clock in the open sea and nearer eight o'clock in the estuary, or even later; for we must allow quite seven hours' ebb to five hours' flow in that funnel in its old unreclaimed state.*[1]

We walked on through the morning, and about midday we saw below us the lonely valley, and in it a hamlet. We said what luck it would be if we chanced to find an inn in this serene place, and we recalled just such a discovery as this by the wayside, miles from anywhere; an inn with a gracious hostess who came through her little garden to welcome us, and roasted a fowl for us. "Bear" Warre was with us, and each of us accused the others for many months after of having fallen in love with the handsome woman who had welcomed us. In this valley, too, a welcome awaited us. We found a small, ugly, newly built hotel, kept by an Englishman. We were the only visitors, and it was one of the most silent places I ever was in. Belloc was delighted with it, and I expected he would

[1] *Six British Battles.* (Arrowsmith: 1931.)

vote for staying the night there. But after an excellent lunch, we walked on again through deep woods. The next year we returned with the Allisons, and spent a night in the hotel.

He has described in one of his essays[2] how he found another little village with an inn—the Place of Peace he called it. He slept in a room with heavy curtains, with a window from which he could see the hills, and at night there was the sound of a stream. And there he stayed for three days, "reading the life of Bossuet, and writing a little verse, and often wandering to the small waterfalls and tarns in the uplands of that countryside." Then he says: "But on the fourth day I thought I would be gone. One should not tempt such things or abuse the gift of them. If too great beauty and too great intelligence are dangerous, and certainly too great wealth, and even perhaps too great bodily well-being, then blessed Peace must not be over-indulged." Well, that is the literary way of putting it. But I will warrant it was our old friend la Bougeotte (the hussy!) at her tricks again. Loneliness may have had something to do with it, but even when he had a companion he could not remain long in one place. In this instance, however, I believe that there may have been something besides restlessness and loneliness to drive him on. He did really feel, as he says, that we harried mortals must beware of the Place of Peace. It must be taken as a blessed interlude, but to make it an excuse for shirking the burden of life is not only a peril to the soul, but may lead to the loss of human dignity and of personal honour. Such things, when they come our way, are outside the context of our lives. They are like visions, and the memory of them remained with Belloc through the years; so that when he did find a place of quiet and calm, he had the strength of

[2] *A Conversation with a Cat.* (Harper: 1929.)

mind to tear himself away from it. And the abandonment
of momentary content was made easier by his natural restlessness.

*   *   *   *   *

At various times we went to Rocamadour, and to Rennes
and Nantes (to buy wine), to the battlefield of Agincourt,
to Montreuil, to Lisieux, to Provins, to the gorges of the
Orne. I recall a very lively lunch with Sisley Huddleston,
whom we had met by chance in Rouen. We had been sailing, and were on the way back to the *Nona.* I read some
years later in one of Huddleston's books a description of
the lunch, in which he said how he had thought, that
night, of us brave fellows being tossed about in a moun-
tainous sea. But the brave fellows were snug in their beds
on land that night. There was also a meeting with D. B.
Wyndham Lewis at St. Germain. Belloc had a great admiration for him, and said he was the wittiest man he
knew—an opinion in which he was by no means alone.

Looking back now on my good fortune I ask myself
what it was that made Belloc such an unparalleled travelling companion. The life abroad was always strenuous,
the demands made on the intellect were heavy, and one
had to accustom oneself to his habits, which were unlike
those of other men. Partly, of course, my contentment was
due to my liking and disliking many of the things he liked
and disliked. We were of the same religion, we both detested modern life with its noise and—rush; as I write the
word I smile. We were always rushing, but somehow, it
was not in the least like being with a hustler. We both
liked wine and food. Again I smile. Meals were often irregular. But when you sat down to a meal you took your
time, and enjoyed it. We both liked walking about towns
on foot—the only way to see them properly. We both liked
history—he to talk of it, and I to listen. Our literary tastes

were much the same. We agreed about Ireland and Poland and Germany, and my love of France dated from the days when I was in Paris with my father and mother, and my nurse used to take me for walks in the Tuileries gardens. We both loved singing in chorus. I dislike visits to museums and galleries, and I was never in my life in either with Belloc. One day in London a friend told us he was going to Madrid. Someone said: "Of course you will go to the Prado." "Of course. I wouldn't miss Velasquez for anything." Belloc moved impatiently. "Oh, anybody can see a Velasquez," he said with scorn. It was not that he did not like Velasquez, but he was afraid that the art-talk was going to start. Also, he would have said there are much better ways of spending the time in Spain than hanging about picture galleries.

Partly, then, my days abroad with Belloc were enjoyable because we had many tastes in common, and held the same opinions on many debated questions. Again, though I have no method in my make-up and am lazy-minded, I can appreciate "staff-work" so long as I do not have to do it. But my happiness in his friendship was based on something more important than community of interest; on the man himself. You could disagree with him, you could be annoyed or fatigued, but you could never be bored. He kept you at your highest potential, physically and mentally. He whipped you up the whole time, transmitted his enthusiasm, and entertained with a mixture of learning, wit, wisdom, fun. How many times I have heard people say: "He needs a Boswell." It would have had to be a very secret and skilful Boswell, for Belloc could never tolerate the idea of hero-worship, and if he had thought that anyone was noting down his conversation, he would have roared with laughter, and given the Boswell something outrageous for his notes. But he would soon have become annoyed, and would have avoided him. He could utter remarks of a Johnsonian rotundity and wisdom, but Boswell would have wearied him very quickly.

Chesterton said that Belloc in low spirits was better company than anyone else in high spirits, and that I think was due to the habit I have mentioned of grumbling with a kind of boyish exuberance, and with a choice of phrase that was entirely his own. His vitality had remarkable effects on other people's low spirits. The late Father Leo Ward told me that once when he was ill and depressed in Paris he met Belloc, and before they parted Father Ward had forgotten his depression and almost believed that he was not ill at all. Belloc could never be inactive, and when we were in a train or a car, he would often spend his time scribbling rhymes or working out some mathematical problem. If he was worried about his affairs, he would work it off in that way, or with some gloomy song with a sting in the tail. He attacked depression in himself and in others with laughter or ridicule, and his "bedside manner," when one was once familiar with it, was not as unsympathetic as a description of it would sound. His conviction that to resent unhappiness is not only unintelligent, but a waste of time, was very salutary.

Grumbling is another matter, and there was something in his grumbling that always reminded me of the two years I spent in the ranks as an infantryman. We all grumbled incessantly, and often in song, but we did not expect that anything would ever be different. We were Fred Karno's army, and we announced it, not with bitterness or anger, nor with a whine, but with full-blooded irony. Even so, Belloc realized that we human beings are Fred Karno's army, and that grousing lightens the pack and shortens the road, and prevents a man from being a prig. When he was depressed, he would say something like this: "We will now go into this filthy, stinking, accursed den of thieves and order one of their abominable meals, or perish miserably in the attempt. Human life, my children, is a disgusting affair, or words to that effect."

He was, even in his travels, a prolific correspondent, and would always write a card or a letter to his friends. It is hardly necessary to say that they were not at all like the conventional cards or letters which most people write. They were often almost illegible, as he would write in a train or a hotel lift, or in any odd place, and put down whatever came into his head. I have before me, as I write, a card from Paris. It says:

> Remark that, like Guy Fawkes's, my writing is uncertain. This is not due to drugs, but to writing standing up in the street. I have just given a poor woman twopence. She gave me this card in exchange. I lose, but gain eternal glory. I have met, officially, 43000000 Frenchmen, including the Cardinal Archbishop. I long for dear old England.

A card from Marseilles, where he had just landed from a boat, says:

> At 9.30 to 10 a.m. on 1/XII/'27 I saw the great Canigou right abeam to port on the course from Minorca to Marseilles, I suppose 90 miles away? Anyhow, a record. I'll measure it when I get back to Chartres.

Another card, written when he was going to sea, has no beginning or end. Across it, in large letters, is "Me for the Salt!", and then:

> Home they brought her warrior dead,
> With his belly full of lead.
> Pity they could not contrive
> To bring her warrior home alive.

From Bressuire in the Vendée he writes:

> All the people and animals here go to Mass. So the Masonic Town Council calls the streets by all the atheist

names it can think of—which isn't many, for they know little.

And from Brussels:

Here I sit, just on the spot where the detestable Hoorn millionaires had their traitorous heads chopped off: would they had caught the ringleader, William of Orange, but he lived on to do untold evil with his vast fortune, and to ruin Christendom and the poor. It is an afternoon of Paradise. No noise in the great square, soft sunlight and excellent white port at 4½d the large glass.

From Constantine he writes: "Tomorrow I get to the edge of the sand. I complete James II." And I remember Robert Lynd telling Belloc after lunch one day that he had seen an enthusiastic review of his *James II*. Belloc replied: "The fool would have been even more enthusiastic if he'd known it was written in the desert."

From Messina:

The rebuilding of Messina since the earthquake is most remarkable. But perhaps you have seen it. I saw two men in a boat struggling with Charybdis this morning. It has become a piffling little eddy. I'm for Athens.

From Rome he sends me a frightful, gaudy picture of a vulgar slut, who is meant to be entrancing.

Bear thinks this beautiful. But I say it's an association of ideas, because she was Kind to him. I found her rather empty-headed, and not really well-bred, not exactly a lady.

He writes from Portofino:

(1) Do me a favour and post this, enclosed, to Jimmy Gunn. It is to ask him to sell me two or three photographs of my picture. I don't know his address—I can't remember the number. Would you add it?

(2) A Sirocco is blowing out of Africa. The Coast of the Mediterranean from Spezzia to Hyères is a mass of swine,

motor-cycles, motor boats making a hell of maddening noise, gramophones and loud-speakers.

(3) I had to come down the coast to get a boat for civilization. I propose to land at Marseilles and strike for the hills beyond the Rhone.

(4) I'll be back some time in October.

(5) I crossed the Apennines on a mule.

A letter to my wife says he is going to Geneva to eat crayfish and laugh at the League of Nations.

It is full of fun. I was there last year when they made an Ex-German-Spy-Lithuanian-lunatic stop by force after he had spoken 4 hours, very quickly, and in Lithuanian: which, I am told, is a most interesting tongue, resembling Sanskrit. The guzzling at Geneva is paid for by you and me. The Authorities have asked Snowden to come back quietly and not to make a fool of himself and his country. There is no other news, except that the "Spectator" has called the Catholic Church a miasma.

✿   ✿   ✿   ✿   ✿

When you had once accustomed yourself to his idiosyncrasies, he was an easy companion. He travelled "rough." There was never any fuss about luggage on our journeys abroad, because we carried what we needed in our hands. The irregularity of the meals, which was often unpleasant for a younger man, was a necessary part of his mode of travel, and it is better to miss a meal than to make a fetish of eating at regular hours, when there is so much to be seen and enjoyed. All he asked of a bedroom was that it should be quiet, and dark. If the curtains did not keep out the light sufficiently, he hung a blanket over the window. When he went to a hotel or restaurant where he was known well, the proprietor would have a talk with him, but there was never any question of his being treated as an important person. He discouraged that kind of fuss if there was any sign of it, with the result that one could eat in peace. As to hotels, he chose, whenever he could, the old-fashioned places—in Dieppe, for instance, the Hôtel du Commerce, which he had known since his youth. The great modern palaces he regarded as examples of the new barbarism, and avoided them, in his own phrase, "like the plague." For, apart from the noise and the railway junction atmosphere, he detested very bright lights. He liked to come to some sleepy old town, not too large, and to sit at a café table talking about its history, its architecture and its people—and always wondering how long it would last before "improvements" ruined it.

He was an expert in little cross-country or mountain railways, and never minded travelling uncomfortably. In England he often astonished someone who was going on holiday in France, by reeling off detailed information about the steam-trams or the small railways in the part of the country the man was going to visit. He travelled always with a purpose, with the result that every day was full of interest, since he usually knew what to avoid. If, by any chance, you came to a place unpleasant or without interest, you were out of it before you had time to be disappointed.

I find it remarkable that one whose talk was so full of foreboding and of distaste for the age in which he lived should have been such an exhilarating companion. One would have thought that his gloomy view of the present and of the future would have had a depressing effect, and would have become tedious. It was never so, because what he had to say was so well worth the saying, and was said in his own distinctive way; and because his moods changed so swiftly. I have often thought that the nearest one could come to giving some idea of the quality of his talk in a café or a train would be to take one of those essays of his, in which the reader is never sure what will come next. Erudition, buffoonery, poetry, scalding mockery are all jumbled up together, and sometimes the mood changes in the middle of a sentence. He rarely talked in the same strain for long, for however serious was his subject, his sense of humour was always on the watch, to pounce. Even when a range of mountains or a broad plain started him on some historical speculation, he would interrupt himself to throw in a riotous remark.

One of the deprivations which must have tried him most sorely was the cutting off of travel during the war, and then, through his increasing infirmity, after the war. At first he would talk of going abroad again, but, as time went on, he accepted the impossibility of travel with resignation, and when his memory became bad, it was of his early days he talked most—particularly of California. His Memoirs, which he had intended to write, would have told us much of those journeys and experiences of his youth, of which there are a few hints in essays and in *The Contrast*. For such a prolific talker, he spoke little of his early youth. One had to question him, and even then, he never seemed inclined to develop the subject. I think he had no idea how interesting any details of his life would have been to other people. I cannot imagine that any other man who had walked from Toul to Rome would have talked so little about it. The discoveries one made about him were haphazard. For instance, he told me one day that he had walked from York to Edinburgh, to take up a tutoring appointment, and that the closing lines of his *Danton* were written while sitting beside a stream on that walk. I realized once in Paris, what I realized far more fully when I read the reminiscences of Mrs. Belloc Lowndes: that Belloc, if he had talked more about himself, could have given a wonderful picture of his early years. We were being entertained by the Dunoyer family. I had no idea at the time that Charles Dunoyer was the son of the Dunoyer who was to be the guardian of the Belloc children, Hilaire and Marie, if both their father and mother died. The family name was Dunoyer de Segonzac, and the Marquis de Segonzac had been guillotined during the Revolution. Anatole Dunoyer de Segonzac became a Republican, and dropped the "de Segonzac." In the next generation the "de Segonzac" was re-adopted, and is the name borne by the well-known painter today. Belloc told me none of this, and it was only when I heard one of the family (of which three generations were present) say, "Last time I saw you, Hilaire, you were riding on an enormous bicycle," and refer to a time long past, that my curiosity was roused. Even so, it was not until I read about these people in "Where Love and Friendship Dwelt" that I knew how they came into Belloc's life. The only time I ever heard him refer to his remarkable Aunt Lily Ballot, he merely said: "She was a most extraordinary woman." Of his grandfather, Hilaire Belloc, he was more ready to talk towards the end of his life.

Looking back on the days I spent travelling with him, I am grateful for an experience I could have had with no other man; for the new things I saw, and for his gift of making more vivid to me the places with which I was already familiar. But above all am I grateful for that merry companionship.

6

THE OTHER SIDE OF THE LEGEND

I, LIKE EVERYBODY ELSE, KNEW THE LEGEND OF BELLOC'S
tempestuous gaiety long before I met him. The legend
persisted because even his cynical utterances and his moments of bitterness were usually mixed with laughter. His
complaints against life were made in such an exhilarating
manner that it was not easy to believe that they were intended to be taken seriously. He was as likely as not to
make fun of his own troubles, and he was as amusing
when he was in a sombre mood as when he was uproarious. An unexpected turn of phrase, perhaps only the
startling use of a word that was ludicrously out of place,
made you doubt whether he was wholly serious, especially as the spectacle of human folly never ceased to entertain him. He could attack savagely in a lecture or a
speech, but he could also use laughter and ridicule as a
weapon. Those who never met him, and knew only his
lighter work, may be excused for accepting the picture of

119

a swashbuckling figure, who spent his time roaring choruses in inns. The man of the open air, the wanderer, the sailor, the singer made a great appeal to young men, more especially in an age when most writers confine their activities to writing, and lead restricted and increasingly uninteresting lives. A clean wind blew through his books, and he made it possible to believe that a professional writer could lead a large and romantic life. The footprints of the "Four Men" could be traced across Sussex, and the walk from Toul to Rome, and a hundred adventures in the mountains or on the seas, contributed to the legend of the happy man who sailed his own boat, composed the music for his own songs, and drew the pictures for his own books.

It was some time before I realized that Belloc was an unhappy and a disappointed man. His habit of expressing his discontents in such an amusing way made it difficult to disentangle the genuine bitterness from the jests. Yet there was no mystery in this seeming contradiction in his character. He was a man of robust health and strong will who, when trapped into exposing his deeper feelings, regained his balance, as it were, before you had noticed what had happened. He enjoyed the good things of life in the heartiest manner, and was far too sane to allow personal grievances or misfortunes to interfere with good company. I remember a man saying to him: "So your old friend Philip Kershaw is dead." He said, "Yes," and was silent for a moment. Then he burst into song, and everyone joined in. That was, I think, the first time that I was not deceived.

I have said that there was no mystery in the unhappiness of a man who seemed so happy. Anyone acquainted with the circumstances of his life must realize this. After a brilliant career at Oxford he was disappointed of a Fellowship. He married young, as a poor man, and had five children. It was soon evident that his books, though they brought him reputation, were not going to earn enough money to give him leisure for the work he wanted to do, the work he thought it his duty to do. Four years in Parliament disgusted him with public life. In middle age, condemned to work harder and harder, he lost his wife, his eldest son and most of his closest friends. Family life, which had meant everything to him, ended when two sons went abroad and a daughter married. Suffering from insomnia and increasing loneliness, he went on producing books and essays and articles year by year.

It is not to be supposed that he talked of his family affairs when he railed against life. His unhappiness was nearly always expressed in general terms. He was very fond of saying, in the merriest fashion:

> I'm tired of love, and still more tired of rhyme,
> But money gives me pleasure all the time.

And most of his grumbling was against "modern life," and the conditions of living—especially noise, the drudgery of writing and his inability to sleep. The grumbling was taken as a joke by his friends, and he himself made a joke of it. I was very surprised when he said to me one day: "Great love is outside the scale of human life. Something always happens. Someone dies. It all ends." And I recall the first time when I saw him really saddened, and with some spring dried up in him. We were staying in a hotel in Lisieux, and after our dinner he fell silent. Then he said: "I came here as a young man with my wife. I was just married. It was in 1896. We stayed in this hotel." The occasion is very vivid to me, because I saw how he still mourned and what the core of his loneliness really was, and because it was perhaps the only occasion when he did not want to talk, but sat quietly with his thoughts of thirty years ago.

But it was not only his private life which brought him

unhappiness. Both as a man and as a writer he was in fierce opposition to the world of his time and, more particularly, to the shallow and absurd philosophy of what was called progress. The triumph of physical science, coinciding with the decay of religion, had produced that mood of arrogance of which H. G. Wells was the most popular exponent. Belloc saw in this baseless confidence in a splendid future, not only lack of intelligence and reasoning power, but immediate peril. In books and articles and speeches he challenged this and all the other popular assumptions of his day. What he had to say was unfamiliar and even grotesque to the majority of his readers, and distasteful to very many. It was not what they were accustomed to reading, nor what they wanted to be told. And as the only way to drive home an unfamiliar truth is to hammer and hammer and hammer away at it, his repetitions, his emphatic manner and his pugnacity irritated people. Particularly irritating to them was his warning that England, which he loved so dearly, was declining, and his insistence that Europe must return to the Faith or perish seemed mere eccentricity to a generation which had taken it for granted that the Catholic Church was moribund. In his championship of Ireland and of Poland, and his refusal to believe in the German "change of heart," he was the voice of an unpopular minority. It was no consolation to him to see so many of his prophecies coming true. The proof that people were too stupid to listen to warnings increased his melancholy, but never broke his spirit. As a duty, and with decreasing hope, he went on with his work. In the field of history he redoubled his efforts. He had set himself the task of correcting Whig, or official history as taught in this country. His theses appeared so strange, and his power of vividly resurrecting the past was so great, that it was easy to suggest a doubt whether this was serious history or mere special pleading.

He himself underestimated the effect of his historical work, which is already visible, and is increasing.

Today we see around us the fulfilment—so soon!—of many of Belloc's forebodings, and we can understand why he was appalled at what he saw coming. We are more than half-way to the Servile State, Europe has broken in pieces before our eyes, England is declining. "Poland is the test," wrote Belloc at the beginning of the second war. Poland was, indeed, the test. As for that dream of progress and of the happier world of the scientists, the awakening could not have been more unpleasant. Other men saw what was coming, but Belloc's was the eloquence and the untiring energy which persisted, in the face of indifference, and he should be honoured, in time to be, as one who saw more clearly than the statesmen; who was wise long before the event; whose courage deserved more recognition than it has had.

✿　　✿　　✿　　✿　　✿

It chanced that this man, whose convictions in the field of public affairs and international questions were so strongly opposed to the generally accepted ideas, was destined to be the champion of the Catholic Church in this country. Once more, and this time in that department of his work which was by far the most important, he was in a minority. Once more he had to fight ignorance, indifference and active resentment. But there was a special circumstance which made his burden heavier, and his disappointments harder to bear. That special circumstance was the lack of support from his fellow-Catholics, who had grown accustomed, in Belloc's youth, to being regarded as the adherents of a foreign sect, a little band of eccentric people who clung to a dying religion. They were permitted to practise that religion, and in return for good-humoured tolerance they considered it their duty to go on their way quietly, without calling too much attention to themselves. So it was that Belloc went into battle a leader without an army. But that was not all. It was not merely that, with honourable exceptions, he had no support. He met even hostility from those who should have supported him. The vigour of his polemics and apologetics made them uncomfortable and uneasy. They would not have denied that what he was saying was true. But was it wise to say it quite so loudly and so often? Would not this militancy make more enemies than friends? By calling attention to the Church so peremptorily, and telling people that it was very much alive, would not this combative figure make the Church even more unpopular than she was? Was it not better to keep quiet until attacked? Some words in *The Cruise of the "Nona"* illustrate Belloc's attitude to religious controversy.

> The orthodox seem to feel, in approaching the sceptics, that they are dealing with superiors. It ought to be just the other way. The people who are in the tradition of Europe, who have behind them the whole momentum of civilization, who have humour and common sense as the products of Faith, ought to approach their contradictors as inferiors.

Such words were not guaranteed to make him popular. There is still today a difference of opinion about Belloc's aggressiveness. For myself, I think we Catholics got a far better leader than we deserved. In any case, he was a fighter by temperament, and he could not have borne witness to the truth in any less full-blooded way. It required great courage for a man who had to earn his living by his pen, to risk antagonizing people by his pride in something they knew little of, and that little in a distorted way. But it required still greater courage to meet the disapproval of those on whose behalf he was making such prodigious efforts. I quote some words which Mr. F. J. Sheed wrote of him when he died:

> More than any other man, Belloc made the English-speaking Catholic world in which all of us live. There was Chesterton, of course, but then Belloc had so much to do with the making of Chesterton, and Chesterton not much with the making of Belloc.

What Belloc wanted to make people understand was that it is those outside the Church who are eccentric, abnormal in the life of Europe. He certainly helped many to find the Church, and forced his contemporaries to take notice of her. But he well understood—and this again troubled his mind and saddened him—that "peril to the soul," as he put it, "through hatred," which is a risk run by one who is perpetually at war with his time, and is fighting to achieve victory, and not merely to enjoy an argument.

Fortunately, his never-failing sense of humour and his capacity for enjoyment did a great deal to counterbalance the anxieties and disillusionments of his public career. Even so, what is remarkable is that he could recover so rapidly from a mood of discouragement, and put aside, with such apparent ease, the troubles that never left him. His strength of will and courage of heart were a part of his greatness. It may be said that he had grown used to being in a minority, having been in early youth an anti-Dreyfusard, and later, a pro-Boer. But when one is young there is something romantic in battling against heavy odds, and being on the unpopular side. As one grows older, and responsibilities increase, it becomes a more serious matter. There are bound to be wakeful moments in the night when repeated effort without result (as it seems) takes on the appearance of futility, and the whole purpose of one's life is called into question. Belloc knew how to treat such momentary weaknesses, and he laughed them out of his life and out of his work.

His wide experience of men and things had given him a justifiable contempt for the intelligence of professional politicians; his contempt for their motives was not always justifiable. But no man had a clearer idea of what was happening, between the wars, to England and to Europe. For he not only wrote lucidly. He thought lucidly. Many of his friends believed that he took too gloomy a view of the international situation, but they would hardly say that today. They found him obsessed with the peril to England of imitating German social legislation, and his campaign for a wider distribution of property, which alone could make the poor man independent, seemed to them an impracticable dream. To the general public, it seemed the attempt of cranks to "put the clock back," and to interfere with what they had come to regard as a natural law by which everything must get better and better. Scientific discovery was their guarantee that what was called progress was inevitable, and thoroughly to be desired. A man, engaged in such a battle with some hope of success, would be a happy man; Belloc was too clear-sighted to entertain any easy hope. But he regarded it as a duty to stand to his guns. The work wearied him, and the failure of his hearers to understand what he was saying disgusted him. He wanted money for a secure and less laborious old age, but the mere earning of his living became a problem.

The late A. G. Macdonell, writing of Belloc's prose, said: "You may passionately disagree with what he says, you may stubbornly disbelieve what he says, but at least you know with certainty exactly what it is he is saying." Macdonell overestimated the intelligence of Belloc's readers. The remarkable fact is that, in spite of his clarity, people continually misunderstood him. Many misunderstood even *The Servile State,* one of the most clearly and patiently and closely reasoned of all his books; and they went on misunderstanding his meaning even after he had written a preface to a new edition, to correct some of the misconceptions he had noticed. After his death an obituarist went so far as to call him a bigot, that is, a man governed by blind and unreasoning zeal, which was surely an example of misunderstanding run mad. When he said that patriotism was the religion of the English, it was in vain that he praised that patriotism for its power to unify in moments of crisis. His arguments in *The Jews,* and his denunciation of those who hate them and ill-treat them, in *The Catholic and the War,* did nothing to destroy the popular idea that he was an "anti-Semite." When he said that only a wider and more equitable distribution of property could guarantee the independence of the ordinary man, he was accused of wanting to return to the Middle Ages of his imagination. When he said that it was the aristocratic tradition which had made England, he was told that he hated democracy. He took the trouble to explain what democracy really means, and how far we were from it in this country, where the machinery of democracy is mistaken for the thing itself. And the hard truths he told hid from eyes blinded by self-delusion the fact that he was one who loved England with all his heart. It is not difficult for a man to meet the antagonism of people who dislike what he is trying to do, but it is another matter when he is misrepresented. One needs a stout courage to continue the fight.

Any attempt to save men from themselves demands some response from those men, some effort on their part, or, to put it at its lowest, those whom you are trying to help must want to be helped. What Belloc knew, and what would have made a lesser man abandon the effort, was that people not only did not want to be awakened, but resented the idea that there was any need for an awakening. They liked being told what they wanted to believe, and, after a war, were in no mood for unpleasant truths. The immediate problem was day-to-day existence, and the talk of liberty and independence meant nothing, because both were already lost, and most young people had never experienced them. In a time of decline bread will always be preferred to freedom. The Servile State was approaching, but if it was to be a comfortable State, what of it? They had the Hegelian intellectuals to support them, and to talk to them of loss of human dignity was to talk a foreign language. It was, in a phrase of John Phillimore which Belloc loved to quote, "like reading Theocritus to a cow."

❂   ❂   ❂   ❂   ❂

Belloc's temper was sceptical. He never believed anything because he wanted to believe it, or because believing it would make a more pleasant atmosphere for the mind. Many ardent Catholics thought and said that there were signs that England was returning to the Faith. He saw no such signs. There was no flicker of a popular movement in any such direction. There were individual converts, whose numbers were probably balanced by those who lapsed. What would have made him "sit up and take notice" was a whole body of converts in some small town or village. He saw no evidence that the Faith was making any impact in such places, and because of this he underestimated the effect of his own work for the Faith. It produced no movement, but it made everyone aware that the Church was not a decaying survival, but was very much alive in their midst. They might have no sympathy with it, they might even hate it, but Belloc made it impossible for them to ignore it.

Again, he watched the throwing away of our victory in the 1914–18 war, the refusal to listen to Foch, the sneaking admiration for Germany breaking out again in England, the Prussian "change of heart," the fear that France might be too powerful, the swindling of France over the Rhineland. Often I heard him argue with people who wanted to think that the official attitude to Germany was the right one, and when he would say, "Nothing will ever destroy the admiration of the English for the Germans," there would be a hot denial. It wasn't that they loved the Germans, but this time the Germans really were penitent, and were going to behave themselves. Was not Stresemann a good European? And so on. People would say, "Oh, of course Belloc has the French idea of the Germans," as though the French idea of the Germans was self-evidently the wrong one. The French idea of the Germans was that unless you made yourself too strong for them to attack you, they would most certainly attack you. The English idea was that if you made yourself strong, you were provoking them to attack you, and if you allowed the French to be strong, they would be too powerful in Europe, and would upset the "balance of power." The logical result of such a doctrine was the clamour for disarmament, and the abuse of the French for not being enthusiastic about disarmament. Belloc, with his French blood, and the traditions of his French family, knew the truth about the Germans: that they do not change. It was comforting to persuade oneself to the contrary—for a time. But Belloc would have nothing to do with such puerile delusions.

Belloc's dislike of what he saw coming was not confined to the decline of England, and the European chaos. The conditions of modern life were repulsive to him. He who loved human noise, and the hurlyburly of a happy company, could not tolerate the racket of motor traffic and the mechanical din of big hotels and restaurants. He made a hobby of "collecting" quiet places at home and abroad, and his memory for his discoveries was amazing. When I

was going to stay in a hotel on my way to Ireland, he said
to me: "Ask them for room number——" (I have forgotten
the number). "It's at the back, and very quiet." He always
kept such details in his mind, and it was delightful to hear
him telling somebody who was going to France where to
stay in such-and-such a town, what wine to drink, and
what buildings or monuments to note. He would even tell
you how to arrive at a place so as to get the best general
view of it. "Don't come in by train. Get out at ——, and
walk in from the west." I tried many experiments when
travelling abroad alone, and I never found him wrong. He
returned again and again to his favourite quiet places, always with the fear that they might have been ruined since
his last visit; to Vire in the Bocage, to Spires, to St. Valéry-
sur-Somme, to Ribas, where you hear the torrent all night,
and to a hundred others. I told him once to go to a remote
village in the Jura which I had discovered, and he sent me
a postcard when he got there, telling me that he had liked
it so much that he had broken his rule, and stayed there a
whole day and a night. His restlessness was a part of his
unhappiness.

He was unable to accustom himself to the unceasing din
which most people today take for granted. I remember his
exasperation when even the silence of Shipley was shat-
tered by a postman on a motor-bicycle. But at Shipley he
had the repose which he needed. Sometimes on summer
evenings when I stayed with him at King's Land thirty
years ago, we used to have our coffee and liqueurs on a
little table in the garden. The only sounds were the far-off
bark of a dog or the good night of a man going home along
the lane. It was easy to see how much good the peace did
him, healing his fretted nerves, and giving him a brief
interlude before he rushed off again. Before going to bed
he always signed with the Cross the door of the room in
which his wife had died, a room that was never opened,

and then went into the chapel to say his prayers. Occasionally he spoke of her and of their life together, but only
like a man thinking aloud. I have heard many people say
that he should have abandoned the outward signs of
mourning—such as the black-edged note-paper which he
always used, and his black clothes. These things are the
business of the bereaved, and of nobody else. Nor is a
generation which dispenses almost entirely with outward
signs of respect for the dead likely to understand such
matters.

* * * * *

At a first glance, then, Belloc was a happy man. It was
obvious that he enjoyed life. But Monsignor Knox, in the
panegyric which he preached in Westminster Cathedral,
drew attention to something that was undoubtedly true.
"The undercurrents of his mind were sad, and his face
never looked happy in repose." When he was not in the
midst of laughter and talk, the expression of his face was
not merely pensive, but melancholy, and his eyes, which
could blaze with anger or light up with gaiety, were the
eyes of a man who had suffered. His dislike of being alone
can be explained partly by his unhappiness, but more, I
think, by the capacity he had for enjoying discussion and
comradeship. He had a very wide circle of friends, in
whose houses he often worked. In the early twenties,
King's Land, which had been full of his children and their
friends and his friends, could be no longer the centre of
the family life he loved so much. He had to rearrange his
life, and as he was a man of habit, and one who deplored
change and separation, it was difficult for him. He did not
regard it as normal for a man to be much alone. On an occasion, in later years, when my wife was abroad, and I was
unable to join her, I was surprised to find myself bored (a
new experience for me), at a loose end and disinclined to

make any effort. I told Belloc this, and he said: "I know all about it. It is astonishing how lonely a married man is without his wife, how pointless everything seems. I used to feel exactly as you do now."

The fact that this man, who was essentially unhappy, appeared before the world as one who enjoyed life, and became in his lifetime a legendary figure of merriment, of laughter and tearing high spirits, must not be attributed to a perpetual exercise of the will. His will was needed from day to day to keep him working, and to deal with his problems. But he really did enjoy life, and when he was in congenial company it was natural to him to be lively and gay, and required no effort. He had an unusually strong constitution, and until his breakdown might be said to have had good health, in spite of his inability to sleep. Many people who met him envied his apparent happiness, for, as I have said, his full-blooded cursing seemed to be merely a part of his joviality. Moreover, his sanity and vigour dispelled gloom or discontent in his companions. It was impossible, when you were with him, to take your daily troubles too seriously. He helped you to recover your sense of proportion, not by lecturing you or by gravely advising you, but by making you laugh at yourself. This does not mean that he was incapable of sympathy in a case of distress. On the contrary, at such times he would take endless pains to be of service.

"It is most important," he said to me once, "not to give oneself occasion for remorse." He himself knew remorse. The task he had undertaken as writer and speaker exposed him repeatedly to the dangers of making uncharitable judgments, and his fighter's temperament inclined him to misread motives, and to be vindictive in a moment of victory. He was well aware of the risks he ran in his controversies, and of his frequent failures to restrain himself. In consequence, he brooded over these failures, and was saddened that the work he had to do so often led to quarrels and estrangements. I remember him saying, as we passed a country house: "So-and-so lives there. I used to go there a great deal, but I can go there no more. There are so many houses where I'm no longer welcome." He saw the problem quite clearly. The work he had set his hand to must be done. It carried with it certain everyday disadvantages, but also the more serious dangers to the soul. The whole thing was his responsibility. If he damaged his soul, there was nobody to blame but himself. So much the worse for him. That's how he would have put it, and it is the only intelligent way to put it. None but a fool could be happy with such knowledge. One of the sayings he admired greatly was St. Thérèse's "If you will the end, you must will the means." In other words, you must take risks, and be prepared to suffer for your beliefs.

In his writings Belloc has told us very little about his private life, and even in his talk, unlike most prodigious talkers, he was reticent on that subject. He rarely uncovered his soul. In moments of intimacy he dropped hints. But one would have to study his work closely and carefully, and to recall brief phrases in his conversation, before getting a clear idea of the part his religion played in sustaining him in his black moments—which grew more frequent as he grew older. In Miss Maisie Ward's *Gilbert Keith Chesterton* there is printed a letter which he wrote to Chesterton in 1907. That letter, written when he was in his thirty-eighth year, is all about Our Lady, who, he says, has never failed him. It reveals something about Belloc which was not easy to discover; his devotion to the Mother of God. And he says that it is the only letter of its kind he has ever written. It was written on an impulse, to help his friend. In that same book there is printed a letter equally revealing, but of a different quality. It is to the same friend, Chesterton, on his being received into the Church.

Belloc was then in his fifty-third year. In this letter Belloc
explains why, although he has lost the capacity for religious emotion which he once had, through grief and loneliness, he is all the more ready to affirm his faith, "as a
wounded dog, not able to walk, yet knows the way home."
And he says: "I know, without feeling (an odd thing in
such a connexion) the reality of Beatitude." It is not such
an odd thing. Aridity, the absence of natural joy or consolation in the practice of religion, the apparent indifference
of God, are, fortunately for so many of us, no obstacle to
full belief and trust and confidence. They make life hard,
but properly understood, they are a test. What Belloc dis-
closes here is that by the use of will and intelligence he is
able to face suffering and disappointment, not only without loss of hope, but with his faith strengthened. To understand Belloc fully, to get any picture of him in right
proportion, it is essential to know from what source he
drew his steadfast courage, what it was that made him so
persistent and so enthusiastic a champion of unpopular
causes, what was the driving force in him, what alone explains him. His religion, as he said, was not a theory, not a
mood, nor a wonderful story. It was Reality, a Thing.

*   *   *   *   *

In September 1932 Belloc sustained a violent shock. I
knew nothing of the matter, as he did not speak of it to me,
either then, or afterwards; nor, as far as I know, to any of
his friends. He had a strong sense of responsibility, and,
with an unmarried daughter to support, he had to do what
he could for other members of his family. His watchful
care over them all was an added burden, and one that he
never shirked in the slightest degree. It may be asked why,
in these circumstances, he was always going off on his
travels. The answer is that his journeys abroad served a
double purpose. They were essential to his work; to his

books, his lectures, essays, articles. They were also essential as refreshment for his mind. In the midst of research and the collection of material for his work, he could recuperate from his fatigue for a few hours in some quiet place. But it was always a question of how much longer he could continue at such unnaturally high pressure, now that he was in his sixty-third year. He could see nothing before him but excess of work. He knew quite well that he was overstraining himself, but he had always relied on his strong constitution to pull him through. Many years before, when Desmond MacCarthy said to him, "You must be a very happy man," he had replied, "No. Only a very healthy one." Now, in September, the shock came. He wrote to his son Peter:

> . . . It was a dreadful thing that happened. I completely lost my memory. I had a very bad night, and when I got up this morning, I was rather dazed and I remained so during the morning. I tried to do some work in the library of the Reform Club, and I went on till half-past one, and then went off to lunch with my mind quite empty. This sort of thing has happened to me once or twice in the last two or three years. It does not seem to get more frequent, but it is really alarming when it does happen, and distresses me a great deal. It comes of having done more work than I ought to have done at my age.

His powers of recovery and his ability to enjoy life were so great that he was able to go on as though nothing had happened. But the unpleasant experience was a warning, and the possibility of its recurrence must have been a constant dread, especially during the long hours of nights without sleep. Such an occurrence is highly disturbing and even terrifying to one who has no particular troubles, and can afford to take things easy for a while. To a man in Belloc's position the shock cannot be exaggerated, and it requires little imagination to realize what his nights of insomnia must have been like after this experience. It was not the first time it had happened, as he says in his letter, but it was evidently more serious and disturbing this time. After such a shock, one waits for a recurrence, never knowing when the blow may fall. I have more than once insisted on his courage. Until I read this letter to his son, I had not known what was, perhaps, the gravest of all his anxieties—the fear that one day his memory might be permanently damaged. It is little wonder that his dislike of being alone increased; or that he was writing harder than ever. He was writing against time. But to those meeting him casually, he still gave the impression of a happy man.

7

THE INCREASING STRAIN

In the nineteen thirties, Peter Belloc and his wife were settled in Berkshire, and my wife and I in London. The young men and girls of the Rodmell days were married, and the old uproarious meetings became rarer. Belloc, of course, made the round of the houses, and, at one time or another, we all went to King's Land. He was now driving himself harder than ever. He saw old age ahead of him, with no prospect of an easier life, and he was increasingly worried about his inability to sleep. He was at this time nearly always correcting proofs during lunch. In the evenings he would often come to our house, looking very tired, but as full of brilliant talk as ever, when the initial grumbling had died down, and he could forget what he called the "filthy trade of writing." He rarely had a set meal with us. He might have a plate of soup, and sometimes he would ask for a dish of macaroni. But he often produced a huge hunk of bread from a pocket of his cloak,

and asked for some ham. With this and wine he was contented. But just as we thought he was at his ease, he would
begin to do his telephoning, always insisting on paying for
his calls.

One evening I came home late, and on a little table in
front of him was a pile of silver and coppers. I thought for
a moment there had been card-playing, and that he had
won heavily, but the money, my wife explained, was for
innumerable telephone calls. He would reckon what he
owed with the most scrupulous care always, and on one
occasion in Rouen he whispered loudly to me during
Mass: "I owe you fifty centimes on those last drinks."

One night after the three of us had been to a theatre he
came back to our house, and my wife reminded him that
he had forgotten to sign the copy of *Belinda* which he
had given her. When it was produced he read passages
from it, laughing loudly at the farewell of Horatio to the
shores of England: "Adieu! Adieu! Tall cliffs of Albion
. . . Fade, fade, O Shores of my Country!" He told us
that he could get no publisher to take the book, and had
finally published it at his own expense. It took him five
years to write, and it was jotted down on bits of newspaper
and on the backs of envelopes. When the proofs were sent,
the printers had made all kinds of amusing queries in the
margins. "Surely," was one query, "a common sailor would
never have said this." Shortly after *Belinda* had been completed, Belloc and Chesterton and Desmond MacCarthy
and I were lunching at the Gourmets. MacCarthy was at
that time editing a literary magazine, and every time the
talk turned to this magazine, Belloc said: "You must print
Belinda." MacCarthy asked what length it was. "That is
of no consequence. You must print *Belinda*." And so it
went on, and as far as I recollect, MacCarthy did print it.
Anyhow, Belloc was very fond of the book. It is a mistake
to think that it is all pastiche. Jostling the most amusing

parodies of the idiom of another day are passages of great beauty, and before you have finished laughing, you are deeply moved, and then you are laughing again. The description of Horatio and Belinda falling in love is exquisitely done. So is the yearning of old Sir Robert to go back through the years, when he meets his first love, and she replies: "We have been living once again, in a brief moment of reminiscence, a long-dead youth, but our habitation is now fixed in age. Its tedium, its backward gaze upon the past, may be shared in friendship. But the sanctity of that friendship will be the better preserved if we speak no more upon the matter which stirred us both like music—long ago; if we pursue no more that road which, a lifetime since, was closed on us by Providence. We may, without fail, be companions, our lives adjoining yet unfettered; for the rest, that seeming-far, that decorous relation can well sustain us, nor injure the prospect of the living, nor anger our dead, nor ape the irrecoverable days that never can return."[1]

Belloc stayed late that night and talked of some romantic novel of the day. He said: "The mistake these authors make when they write about the love affairs of what is called 'Society,' is that they make their characters romantic. It isn't like that at all." Of another book of the same kind he said: "What a monument to the futility of human life." Before he left us, as often happened, he asked for a large bit of bread to take away with him. "It's in case I can't get to sleep," he said. "It helps me to sleep."

It was characteristic of his restlessness that he rarely appeared to be taking his ease. He was incapable of "relaxing." Sometimes he would sink back in a chair and, with a peculiar gesture, rub the palm of his right hand upwards over his face, from chin to forehead, as though brushing away fatigue, and then close his eyes for a few moments,

[1] *Belinda: a Tale of Affection in Youth and Age.* (Harper: 1929.)

while he went on talking. Then he would sit up, take out his watch, make a calculation, and ask to use the telephone. When he came to see us in the evenings, he always kept his cloak on, having thrust his soft black hat into a pocket of it. His eyes showed his weariness, but his brain was never inactive, and if he lay down full length on a sofa, he took part in whatever was being talked about. He was always worried if he thought he was putting anyone to the smallest trouble. To call him considerate would be an understatement, and he was so humble about himself that it never seemed to occur to him that he was conferring pleasure by a visit. He regarded himself as a nuisance, because his habits did not fit in with other people's, and he never took it for granted, even with close friends, that he would be welcome whatever time he came, and whatever his mood. When he rang up to propose himself for an hour or two, he had to be assured that he was not putting anyone out. I have said something of his habit of incessant telephoning. When his son-in-law, Reginald Jebb, was received into the Church at Haverstock Hill, my wife was his godmother. As soon as the ceremony was over Belloc was heard saying to Father Vincent McNabb: "Father, have you a telephone here? I must telephone."

Sometimes he would break out as he came into the room, "The rich are really extraordinary people," and proceed to relate something said or done by friends of his, adding: "But I like them. I get on with them. I don't belong, but I like their company." It was the same with Americans. He always made fun of them, but he always said frankly that he liked them very much, because they are simple people. As to "the rich," by which he meant well-born people of assured position, there was nothing snobbish in his friendship with them, since he never allowed such friendship to have the slightest influence on his opinions or his conduct. He had no illusions about them.

The one good he saw in being what he called a "hack" was that it left him freedom to move about. As he wrote in an essay, "On Writing as a Trade"[1]: "A couple of years ago I wanted to write about James II. I went off to the edge of the Sahara desert and wrote the book in not many consecutive days in a jolly little bungalow hotel I know of on the banks of a stream coming down from Aures. Now I could not have edited a paper, built a house, audited an account, or acted the part of Hamlet (before paying audiences) in that remote residence by the palm grove. So God be praised! But in that book there were innumerable slips of the pen and half a dozen good, honest howlers, the fruits of hermitage and liberty." The remarkable thing was that, with all his rushing about, his frequent journeys abroad, his social engagements, he retained his powers of concentration on a piece of work which had to be done, and the mere list of his books in these years, apart from his journalistic work, makes an extraordinary catalogue. In 1930 he published *Richelieu, Wolsey, New Cautionary Tales,* and *The Man Who Made Gold* (a novel). In 1931 came *A History of England* (Vol. IV), *Cranmer, Essays of a Catholic Layman in England, A Conversation with a Cat* (Essays), *On Translation* (the Taylorian Lecture), the poem "In Praise of Wine," and a commentary on Allison's *Travel Notes on a Holiday Tour in France.* In 1932 were published: *Ladies and Gentlemen* (verses), *Napoleon* and *The Postmaster-General* (a novel). In 1933: *William the Conqueror, The Tactics and Strategy of the Great Duke of Marlborough, Charles I;* and so on. And this list omits several pamphlets.

❀ ❀ ❀ ❀ ❀

[1] *A Conversation with a Cat.* (Harper: 1931.)

In October 1931 Belloc took me as his guest to the dinner of the Saintsbury Club, where we drank, among other wines, the Latour of 1878—an amazing experience. Belloc rose to the occasion with a magnificent speech, which Maurice Healy, no mean judge of oratory, said was the best speech he had ever listened to; and he deplored the fact that no record of it was kept. As a speaker Belloc was unpredictable. Often he was very tired when he spoke, and sometimes the subject bored him, but even on those occasions there was always some flash of irony or wit, or some piece of wisdom casually dropped. When he put forth his strength, to do justice to a great occasion, he was a first-rate speaker. He was also very effective when he was angry. When the occasion called for a grave and formal speech, he spoke with weight and dignity. In less formal speeches he could become like a mischievous undergraduate, and I have heard him "rag" an audience, to the mystification of some and the delight of others. He appreciated to the full a joke against himself. At a Catholic dining-club the guest of honour was some high foreign dignitary of our Church. Belloc made a vigorous attack on the English Press. When the guest rose, he opened his remarks by saying that one of the things he enjoyed when he came to England was the English newspapers. He then praised them for some time. Either he had not understood Belloc's speech, or he had an excellent sense of humour. His manner was suave and quiet, and I could detect no hint of satire. Anyhow, Belloc enjoyed the joke immensely, and often told the story.

One of the best lectures I heard him deliver was on the Art of Biography, and I wondered at the time to what extent he had prepared it. On going through my papers after his death, I found a sheet of Reform Club notepaper with some scribbling on it. On one page is written, in column form: Slides. Port. Regnier. Bags. Almonds. Ham. Money.

Maison Dorée. Then two telephone numbers and an address. Overleaf is a sketch of a man in a top hat. And then the notes for the lecture, in pencil. Biography:—a Department of history. You represent a man to his fellowmen. What select? (I) That which will explain his motives. (II) That which will explain his effect. (I) In *all* you must select typical action. (II) In (illegible) public action you must select his part therein. The rest—a dozen words or so—is illegible. It was all obviously jotted down at the last moment, in the midst of doing a dozen other things.

A lecture which I regret missing was his Taylorian Lecture of 1931, printed by the Clarendon Press. It is one of the best things he ever did, and from it we learn that he had begun a translation in prose of the Song of Roland, but feared he would never finish it. Two of his best books were based on lectures—*Europe and the Faith*—these were delivered to St. Thomas's Historical Society—and *The Crisis of our Civilization*, containing his lectures to Fordham University during his visit to America in 1937.

A subject that always interested him was fame. He liked to speculate about it, and to discuss whether, as one grows older, the desire for fame grows less. He always said that for an author to be conceited about a piece of good verse or prose only made him ridiculous, because he is a mere instrument. He is inspired from outside, and must not take all the credit for his work. Yet, although the rational part of him despised fame, he recognized ambition, especially in youth, as a necessary driving force, and was, to the end of his life, unable to abandon wholly the very human wish that his poetry might survive. At a dinner given for his seventy-first birthday, in answering a speech in which Duff Cooper had praised his work, and prophesied survival for it, he said that he would be proud if he could know that his work might one day belong to the great treasury of English literature. But it was the fate of his verse which interested him most.

If you talked about his prose, he was always careful to distinguish prose from rhetoric. He knew he could write first-rate rhetoric, but seemed always to be doubtful about his prose. He said to me once, when we were talking about his work: "What I have is a sense of rhythm." He certainly had. He knew how to build up a long passage as though it were a piece of music—with a quiet opening, the development of a theme, working up to a climax, and then the solemn conclusion. The importance of style in writing could not, in his opinion, be overrated, and he always said that literary work, if it is to endure, must be carved in hard material. "So-and-so," he would say, "doesn't know how to construct a sentence." Tricks in writing he abominated, particularly false rhetoric; the depraved habit of feigning an emotion that is not felt, of trying to excite yourself and the reader by making a mockery of what, when it is sincere and honest, can be so noble. Not only does such fustian fail of its purpose, but it puts an indignity on the perpetrator. The trick of epigram or sham epigram he also abhorred. When he used the epigram it was because it was the shortest and clearest way of conveying his meaning. Nor did he ever make a parade of vocabulary, to startle the reader. He used words to instruct, persuade or entertain, but never to "show off." He never "wrote down" to his readers to please or flatter them, but solely to explain something to them as simply as possible. Though he liked to play the fool in his lighter writings, turning somersaults, insulting the reader, grimacing, yet he always had himself well in hand. Indecency he never permitted himself in his writing, though his talk among men was often bawdy. He called the filthy novels of our time "Gloomy dirt," and he said: "Sex is a matter either for privacy or for laughter."

While I was helping him to correct the proofs of a novel

at King's Land one day, he read out a sentence which ended, "Said she, archly," then paused. "Shall we put 'Damn her!' in brackets?" he asked. I said, enthusiastically, "Yes." But he wouldn't do it. Not because it would "destroy the illusion," as the critics say, but because he thought it an excess of clowning.

The desire for fame he regarded as an almost universal and rather ridiculous weakness of human nature, yet a very necessary weakness, if good work is to go on being produced. Though he made no secret of his own hope that his verse, if nothing else, would survive, he treated the whole matter in a healthy, light-hearted way, quoting a wise man who, when asked if he expected his verse to procure him enduring fame, replied: "I shall have as much fame as a dead man wants." He advised those with a craving for fame to flatter the young, who, "in middle age, invariably revere those who praised them in youth. Thus they create a legend." He often said that literary fame was not worth having nowadays, because of the deplorable standards of taste. He was always highly amused by those writers, especially men and women of mature years, who give themselves sleepless nights over hostile reviews of their books, and he had a proper contempt for the floods of mechanical praise which are poured out week by week. No man was less vain about his own work, but no man had a higher sense of the great tradition of English Letters.

To predict the ultimate fate of a great writer's work is today a more hazardous occupation than it ever was. The caprices of posterity are hidden from us, and there are also the special circumstances of the time in which we live. The number of those who care for good writing and of those who have any standard by which to judge such matters is diminishing rapidly. One department of Letters in which Belloc excelled—the essay—is already out of favour. More than any of his contemporaries, he insisted on the clarity and music of words, at a time when the new experiments relied on obscurity and lack of music. His poetry, which he always called his Verse, is in the tradition of English poetry now being assailed. His prose is full of rhythm, and challenges the stop-short prose admired today. He may have to wait a long time, but I think he is assured of lasting fame, because of what he said, and because of the way he said it.

He was a master of many styles of writing, and each one of them is unmistakable. Everything he wrote bears his impress, and could be attributed to nobody but himself. He never, as I have said, indulged in fine writing for the sake of fine writing, but only when he was moved by his subject. In fact, he had a wholesome contempt for faked emotion, for the deliberate pretence masquerading as the genuine thing. He had the greatest respect for the craft which he cursed so loudly and so repeatedly, calling it a "filthy trade." It was always said that he wrote far too much, and the people who said it were the first to be surprised that he died a poor man. While doing the work that he wanted to do, the work for the restoration of religion and the correction of the accepted view of English history, he had to earn a living.

Many examples of the remarkable sense of rhythm, in which he was unrivalled, can be found in his books. Sometimes there will be a short passage, sometimes a complete essay. Such writing, with Belloc, is never a "purple passage." It occurs only when he is under a profound emotion, and is inspired by a vision of some historical event, by great architecture, by landscape, by memories of youth, by musings on life and on death. This solemn and noble music can be heard in many passages of *The Path to Rome,* and *The Four Men.* Two of the most famous examples, already secure in the treasury of English literature, are to be found in his *Danton.* They were written when he was in his twenties, and, familiar though they will be to those who know his work, I will quote them once again. The first is a threnody for the French Monarchy, the second, the closing lines of the book. They have not been equalled in our time.

> So perished the French Monarchy. Its dim origins stretched out and lost themselves in Rome; it had already learnt to speak and recognized its own nature when the vaults of the Thermæ echoed heavily to the slow footsteps of the Merovingian kings. Look up that vast valley of dead men crowned, and you may see the gigantic figure of Charlemagne, his brows level and his long white beard tangled like an undergrowth, having in his left hand the globe and in his right the hilt of an unconquerable sword. There also are the short, strong horsemen of the Robertian house, half hidden by their leather shields, and their sons before them growing in vestment and majesty, and taking on the pomp of the Middle Ages; Louis VII, all covered with iron; Philip the Conqueror; Louis IX, who alone is surrounded with light: they stand in a widening interminable procession, this great crowd of kings; they loose their armour, they take their ermine on, they are accompanied by their captains and their marshals; at last, in their attitude and their magnificence they sum up in themselves the pride and the achievement of the French nation. But time has dissipated what it could not tarnish, and the process of a thousand years has turned these mighty figures into unsubstantial things. You may see them in the grey end of darkness, like a pageant all standing still. You look again, but with the growing light and with the wind that rises before morning they have disappeared.

❂   ❂   ❂   ❂   ❂

But with the mention of that frozen place there comes a thought older than all our theories—the mourning for the dead. Danton helped to make us, and was killed: his effort has succeeded, but the tragedy remains. The army at whose sources he stood, the captain who inherited his action, were worn out in forging a new world. And I will end this book by that last duty of mourning, as we who hold to immortality yet break our hearts for the dead.

There is a legend among the peasants in Russia of a certain sombre, mounted figure, unreal, only an outline and a cloud, that passed away to Asia, to the east and to the north. They saw him move along their snows through the long mysterious twilight of the northern autumn in silence, with the head bent and the reins in the left hand loose, following some enduring purpose, reaching towards an ancient solitude and repose. They say it was Napoleon. After him there trailed for days the shadows of the soldiery, vague mists bearing vaguely the form of companies of men. It was as though the cannon-smoke of Waterloo, borne on the light west wind of that June day, had received the spirits of twenty years of combat, and had drifted farther and farther during the fall of the year over the endless plains.

But there was no voice and no order. The terrible tramp of the Guard and the sound that Heine loved, the dance of the French drums, was extinguished; there was no echo of their songs, for the army was of ghosts and was defeated. They passed in the silence which we can never pierce, and somewhere remote from men they sleep in bivouac round the most splendid of human swords.

    ❋   ❋   ❋   ❋   ❋

That the man who could write like this could also write *The Servile State* illustrates the extraordinary range of his genius.

    ❋   ❋   ❋   ❋   ❋

If Europe returns to the Faith, I think he will stand out as the principal champion of that, at present, unpopular cause. If, on the other hand, the decline continues, and Europe enters another Dark Age, I think that when the Church has once more saved the remnants of our civilization, and we emerge to build again what has been destroyed, Hilaire Belloc will be looked back upon as the great figure of the period, the polemist who fought with all his strength to divert the catastrophe. In either case, whether he is seen as the leader of the vanguard or the inspirer of the rearguard, he will be saluted as one who challenged the false philosophies, and that mechanical thinking which is all that is left of public opinion. Many people realize today that the tragedy of our time is not the economic chaos, not the bankruptcy of statesmanship and diplomacy, but the loss of religion—a loss that has produced these results. But nobody said this so clearly and so repeatedly as Belloc. The instrument at his command was a prose at once flexible and disciplined. His sentences were built, constructed, properly proportioned. This is as true of his majestic rhetoric as of his logical exposition. When he rises to a great occasion, he does what the poet does; he sets his words to music,[1] making an incantation which rouses an answering emotion in the reader. But his own emotion is controlled. There is no excess. And when the occasion demands, he can appeal to reason in reason's own unemotional language.

❋　❋　❋　❋　❋

He went to America again in 1935, reluctantly, as he now felt the strain of long journeys. He wrote to me from the *Lafayette:*

> I am in the middle of the sea, like Jonah's whale. The ship, though French is got up in the purest Prussian fashion, with lunatic furniture and metal tubing everywhere. But the personnel, being French, are polite and quiet. The food tolerable. The wine is not too dear—some very good from Anjou. It snows hard from the S.W., and is bitter cold

[1] Maurice Baring said that Belloc's sonorous prose was "like the mellow tones of a beautifully played 'cello."

. . . I will write to you from New York, where I shall post this on landing. I can't tell you how funny England looks from all this way off. A chance copy of a London newspaper left lying about on board makes me shout with laughter. There are few travellers. About 50. Of these, 8 black Jews, the rest monsters, and two platinum blondes.

I have omitted from this letter long and detailed instructions for buying a book for his schoolboy godson, Auberon Herbert (then at Ampleforth), whose mother and sister were on board with him. Ten shillings was enclosed, and if there was any change it was to be given to the poor.

From New York he wrote to me at the end of February:

I enclose a cutting about a murder trial which you ought to read through carefully, noting every word. There is not one that the most exuberant would presume to add, or the most fastidious would dare to erase. I addressed a great big audience in Boston, where the Catholics are the huge majority of the people. I am to address another in New York to-night; then I go South to Richmond. And after that I go on to Florida and Cuba. I hope to write to you from the comparative peace of these places. From Cuba I shall take a slow German tug to Spain, there being no other boat available. From Spain I shall go to Marseilles, and then to the Holy Land, if I have the strength. I shall take the road of the Crusaders through Asia Minor and Antioch, if I can. I don't want to write about Jerusalem. It has been too much written up altogether. What I want to write about is the battle of Hattin.

I hope the Great White Port Mystery (for I prefer to call it a mystery rather than a scandal) will be solved without tragedy; or, at any rate, if there is a miscarriage of justice, I hope the Press will get properly excited about it, and that the culprit, having been clearly proved guilty, shall be exonerated.

Did I tell you that Dermot MacCarthy has a friend in Dublin who ordered a pair of boots? When they came, one

was so big that his right foot was lost in it, and the other
so small that he could not get his left foot into it. When he
went to complain, the cobbler said, "Did you ever see any
two objects in nature which were exactly alike?"

As I say, I will write again.

My address is King's Land, where Eleanor forwards as I
travel. Write me the news.

The "Great White Port Mystery" is a reference to some
white port which I had ordered for him in London, and it
had gone astray, and never reached him. His daughter
Eleanor and her husband were now living at King's Land.

At the end of March 1935 he wrote to me from the
Reina del Pacifico:

> I am in the Atlantic; east of the sun (for I have just seen
> it setting), and west of the moon (for that luminary, now
> past the full, is but rising). Also, for that matter, north of
> the Azores, where that detestable, mean and treacherous
> ruffian, Richard Grenville, got caught on the Revenge, be-
> cause he couldn't handle his ship, and missed stays. The
> others got away, and his misadventure is the theme of a
> noble poem. Bad history makes good verse.
>
> It will sound incredible to you, but I am on a Tourist-
> Tripper boat. All around me are the souls of the damned,
> reading old Punches, playing Bridge, and trying to digest
> the worst food ever served.
>
> It happened thus. I was going from Havana to Spain.
> Fighting broke out in Cuba while I was in Florida. Sailings
> were cancelled. They are few, anyhow, from the Caribbean
> to Europe. It looked as though I should have to go back to
> New York and sail from there. Then I heard of a ship full
> of trippers doing a cruise and due to touch at Nassau in the
> Bahamas, and make for Vigo and Santander before reach-
> ing England. Nassau has a Governor, and breathes the
> spirit of Empire. Also a Prince and his bride had just
> landed. But with the courage of a lion I went there, and
> boarded the boat. I have eaten that food for a week—and

now I approach civilization. In the dusk of the day after to-morrow's dawn I look to see the two "flash groups" which mark the entrance to Vigo Bay.

I guess I won't get out there, but go on: to Santander or even to La Rochelle. Then to Marseilles. From Marseilles I ought to go to Syria because the publishers have offered me money to do so, but I am very tired. If I can gather the energy I will go on to Syria after some days at Marseilles. If I find I am too much exhausted for that, I shall crawl back to England.

I want you to do something for me, which I trust is not too onerous. I want you to find out the dates of the Jubilee, so that I shan't tumble into the middle of it. I know what the Dons call "An Inferior Limit." The Boy Skunks light bonfires on May 6th—or rather they are lit by electricity. But what is the "Superior Limit"? What is the last day of the business, the last crowd and push? Can you find that out and let me know? I should be infinitely obliged. Then if I am back, I can make my plans to arrive in peace. If you will post me the information not later than April 4th, I shall get it at Marseilles before I leave, even if I do go East. For I shan't leave until after April 8th. Send me a line, Air Mail, to "Poste Restante, Marseille, Bouches du Rhône."

Tell me all the news. In America one hears none. I mean the news of home. I got here, on board, the radio about the new Prussian General Staff plan for 36 divisions, but that was hardly news, it was bound to come when the Banks made our Government back up Prussia. They will build a fleet next.[1] Great fun. Great sport.

When we meet I'll tell you about America: good people, as different from us as the moon, and getting more different every day, and rapidly.

A priest at Baltimore asked me whether the Faith was not now looked at more favourably in England. I said, "No." He asked me where the chief centre of opposition was, and I said, "Oxford." Then he said, "I see. Something

[1] They did. In June the Anglo-German Naval Treaty was signed.

like the Ku Klux Klan." Also many rich women told me all
about the Royal Family over and over again.

In May 1935, after his return from the East, he wrote to
his son Peter:

> By the print on the envelope which encloses this, you
> might think I was still at sea on the Triestino boat. On the
> contrary, I am on the very top of a mountain, in a rude
> hut. It is in the Vosges, about 30 or 40 miles north of the
> Ballon d'Alsace, where you and Hilary climbed with me
> after the war, and where we saw the whole chain of the
> Alps to the south, made pink by the setting sun. I was in a
> motor 'bus on the way from Colmar to Nancy and so to
> Paris, when I saw this hut on the very summit of the road.
> So I got out, and am going to spend the night here, because
> it is dead quiet, and delicious air, with huge forests all
> around and below, and magnificent views over the French
> plains to the west, and Alsace and the Black Forest beyond,
> to the east. It is about 3000 feet up in the air. I expect to be
> in Paris either the day after to-morrow, the 16th, or Friday
> the 17th. In Paris I shall find a lot of post and hideous work
> in quantities, which I dread, for this enormous journey has
> tired me very much. Apart from two crossings of the At-
> lantic and all the Mediterranean both ways—10000 miles of
> sea, I have been lecturing and writing nearly all the time,
> and I have visited New York, Boston, Philadelphia, Wash-
> ington, Baltimore, Richmond, Miami, Nassau, Vigo, Santan-
> der, St. Sebastian, Bayonne, Pau, Nimes, Marseilles, Aix,
> Cannes, Naples, Messina, Athens, Constantinople, Alexan-
> dretta, Aleppo, Antioch, Latakia, Tripoli, Bayreuth, Damas-
> cus, Nazareth, Jerusalem, Bethlehem, Haifa, Cyprus, Brin-
> disi, Bari, Ravenna, Vicenza, Milan, Bellinzona, Lucerne,
> Mulhouse, and it is not over yet.

He had gone East after all, and the result of the journey
was the two books, *The Battle Ground* and *The Crusade.*
He came back very tired, and I think it was in the later

months of this year 1935 that my wife and I both noticed a change in him. It was nothing much—an increasing fatigue at the end of the day, an anxiety about his capacity to go on working so hard, and always the inability to get a good night's rest. At this time he said repeatedly: "I'm knocked out. I can't sleep." Lying awake at night, he worried more and more about the future. Nobody meeting him casually would have suspected any of this, since his energy was as great as ever, and the courage which kept his spirits high was undiminished. But we who knew him so well were ill at ease. He had left his lair in Kensington some time ago to share a house with Warre in Little Stanhope Street. When Warre moved to Chelsea, Belloc went to his old friend Somers Cocks in Brompton Square. In the evening, when he left our house, I used to go back with him, and once or twice his exhaustion was extreme. Yet the next day, after a bad night, he would have rallied his strength, so that I thought I had been unnecessarily alarmed. He continued to travel, to sail and to turn out books and articles and pamphlets and essays, and soon he seemed to have recovered his health. When I came back from Austria in 1936, I found a letter from him, the gist of which was that he was undertaking still more work, and work which would bring him no money.

When are you back? I want to meet you. I am taking over G.K.'s Weekly in two or three weeks' time, and I want to talk to you about it. I shall of course do all my work for nothing, and so, I am afraid, will other people have to, but it is an opportunity for saying things which the stinking official press will never print—just as the old New Age was, and as the paper was in the old days when I started it. I leave here on July 1st and wander about, but am in touch everywhere with the post; and everything is forwarded. I shall not be going to sea till July 18th, and shall then touch at the lovely little ports of England all full of trippers, petrol, and half-naked women in tights—to use no coarser word.

In this year 1936 he published *The Battle Ground, Characters of the Reformation, The County of Sussex, An Essay on the Restoration of Property,* and a novel, *The Hedge and the Horse.* And he was writing *The Crusade.* Peter Belloc had noticed that he seemed to be overstraining himself, but I think he had no undue anxiety about his father's health, as there were such reserves of strength, and so much liveliness. Moreover, his family and his intimate friends were so accustomed to his complaints about fatigue, that they paid little attention to them. This year he lost another dear friend, Gilbert Chesterton, whom the Belloc children called Uncle Gilbert. Belloc and Peter and I had been over to see him at Beaconsfield, and he, too, was a weary man, but he had not the strong constitution of Belloc. We drank wine and talked, and that was the last time I saw him. I read of his death while I was in an inn on the Brenner Pass.

The lunches at the Gourmets and the dinners at the Escargot continued. One day Peters and I had started our meal, when Belloc arrived a few minutes late. Near us were three very quiet men, evidently discussing something of importanc. From the door Belloc shouted, "Where is the Beast Peter?" The three men obviously thought that this fierce-looking newcomer was threatening one of us with violence. They looked most uncomfortable, and I think they expected one of us to be struck by the thick blackthorn which Belloc carried. However, they were reassured, but still astonished, when he began to talk about Louis XIV. And the Beast Peter came in shortly afterwards. He was at this time roving round the London docks, and had already written those two admirable books, *Below Bridges* and *Tongue Pie,* which are full of the talk and the deeds and misdeeds of the sailors and stokers and bailiffs he met and drank with in the taverns of Wapping and Limehouse. His young family was growing up in the Berkshire village to which he returned every night.

*   *   *   *   *

Belloc went again, and even more reluctantly, to America in 1937. My wife and I went to King's Land to say goodbye to him, and his daughter Eleanor drove him to Southampton. He made no secret of his dread of the long journey, but he was in very good form, and we had the usual noisy meal together. We were now living at Henfield, within ten miles of Shipley.

From New York he wrote to me:

> My one consolation for the dreadful business of lingering on here like a lost soul in Purgatory, at the end of the strain of all this lecturing, is that I have avoided London during this foul period. However, one can avoid London without going to New York. What is the betting that the rearmament programme breaks down before it is completed? I have a growing impression that it will do so, the burden is too great. But we shall see.
>
> Thank you so much for all your trouble about the Hachette book. I will tell my friend over here that it has gone off, and then he will go through the usual fight with the Customs, to try and get it out of their hands. Two copies of "The Path to Rome" which I had sent over here for friends have been held up at the Customs for a fortnight. I can't remember whether your wife was ever over here, as her sister so often is, but if she knows this country she will understand why I want to get back to Europe. I am fond of them and get on with them—but it is like being in the moon.

Belloc got back to England shortly after the Communists had won their great success of the Spanish civil war —a success not of arms, but of propaganda. Writers and speakers in England, many of them honest men who had no idea that their generous emotions were being exploited, had played their part in creating that mood in which large numbers of dupes, ignorant of Spain and of the history of the conflict, were ready and even eager to accept whatever was said against Franco and his fighting men. The lies about Guernica got a good start, and the exposure of those lies aroused little interest.

It had been the custom to talk of Spain as a picturesque survival, a wonderful treasure-house of the Arts, a memorial to a vanished age. The traveller, rambling in the ancient streets of Toledo, had no reason to suspect that what seemed to have died in the Middle Ages had any part to play in the living world of the twentieth century. But what looked like death was only sleep, and the violent awakening reminded progressive Europe that the war against the infidel is never ended. In the old towns historical memories stirred, and the last lines of the greatest of our Christian Epics became news. Charlemagne, weary with cares and with unending warfare, has laid himself down to sleep in his high vaulted chamber. But St. Gabriel who, with St. Michael of the Peril, has borne the soul of Roland to Paradise, appears to the aged Emperor, and bids him raise new armies and ride out once more against the Paynim. Christendom is calling to him for help. And Charlemagne weeps and tears his white beard in anguish. So now the heirs of the Reconquest heard the horn calling:

Roland, mon compagnon, sonnez votre Olifant!

Toledo, for hundreds of years the advanced bastion and bulwark against the Mohammedan, the fortress from which the fighters of Aragon and Navarre and Castile went out to the victory of Las Navas de Tolosa—Toledo entered history once more, and gave to the world for pride the immortal story of Moscardo and the Alcazar.

The challenge of Franco Belloc saw not as an isolated event, but as something which concerned Europe, whose champion Spain had made herself. Nor did he doubt the outcome.

Ganivet finds in Seneca the Stoic a type of the Spanish soul and the hardness and resolution of the Spanish character—that tenacity which brought them triumphantly through the centuries of the Reconquest, and which so deceived Napoleon. It was Seneca's doctrine that a man has in himself, in his soul, a force which is indestructible, and that therefore his duty is to convince himself that nothing from outside can overcome his soul. Add that armour to the armour of the Faith, and you have an explanation of Spanish history. It explains both the heroic patience and the savage cruelty of which the Spaniard is capable—that cruelty which well-meaning supporters of Franco foolishly denied.

Later on Belloc went to Spain, and met Franco, who, he told me, reminded him a little of Foch. He also met the hero of Toledo, Moscardo, and from a Spanish headquarters in a village of the mountains he watched the fighting on the lower Ebro, and heard the news of the break-through which was followed by the last victorious offensive.

He was soon travelling again—to Holland and Ireland and to the Baltic countries. Warre, who had illustrated *Many Cities*, accompanied him to Denmark and Sweden and Norway and Poland, and drew the pictures for *Return to the Baltic*. Warre was one of his closest friends, and was an excellent companion for him, as he took everything calmly, and as they had very many friends in common. Belloc seemed to be in better health at this time. He still complained of loss of sleep and excess of work, and he was, of course, not so active physically as he had been. But his strength of mind and body enabled him to go on writing at the same pace, jotting down bits of books on envelopes and old letters, or even on newspapers. Once when we were going through some papers at King's Land I found several pages torn out of a picture paper—I think it was the *Illustrated London News*. There was writing scrawled all over the pictures and over the margins. "What's all this?" I asked. "Let's have a look," he said. I handed the sheets to him, and he deciphered the writing. "It's part of *The Four Men*," he said. And we found the original sketch of the amusing map of Sussex from that book. He asked me if I would like it, and it now hangs in my study at home.

As he became more unhappy about the international situation, one might have expected to find him in low spirits. This was not so. The "Spouting well of joy within, that never yet was dried," was still there. There crept into his lighter writing a kind of "I give you up!" attitude to the human race. There was an increasing use of slang and of colloquialism, which was not carelessness. He seemed to be saying: "Everything is so abominable and so absurd that we may as well have what fun we can before the whole thing collapses." When he came to Henfield he talked a great deal about March 9th, 1936, the day that might have changed the world, the day on which Hitler walked into the Rhineland, and got away with it. "That is a date to remember always."

He wrote to me that he "had a brief illness" on the trip to the Baltic country, "now, I think past, but disturbing while it lasted, and due to trying to rush about too much in old age." It was useless attempting to induce him to take care of himself. He would not go near a doctor. "At my age, they can only patch you up." His meals were still as irregular as ever. We had once got him to be the guest at a St. Patrick's Night dinner of the National University of Ireland Club, of which my wife, as a graduate, was a member. He had apparently not eaten since morning, and was faint from want of food, but he made an excellent speech to the toast of "Ireland." On another occasion he returned from France in a storm, and had been ill on the boat. He demanded bread and butter and bloater paste and wine, and he ate like a starving man. At King's Land one day he told me he had had an attack of dizziness, and that his father had once had a stroke.

Meanwhile, he watched what was so surely coming, and continued to deplore the folly and short-sightedness of the English educated classes. He saw the cowardly and perilous compromise over Danzig as the blunder which had brought on not only our own troubles, but the dilemma of Poland. Prussian propaganda had succeeded in getting the old Polish province of Pomorze talked of and written of as the "Polish Corridor," and it was a common experience to read that the Corridor ought to be "given back" to Prussia, as though it belonged to Prussia—just as people said later that Ireland should "give back" certain of her ports to England. It was evident that when Hitler should choose his moment to attack Poland there would not be in England the same degree of moral indignation as had been stirred up by the attack on the Czechs. Even if, today, you ask a man "Why did not the Czechs fight?", he will reply, "How could they? What hope had they?" What hope had Poland? Belloc had always been a champion of Poland, the country which all through its early history was the fortress of Christendom, and in 1683 and 1920 saved us all. At Czestochowa, the great shrine in the province of Kielce, they keep in the Pauline Monastery Belloc's "Ballade of Our Lady of Czestochowa," which he wrote out in Latin for the Prior when he was there. But it is at Vilna, when you come to the Ostra Brama, with the little chapel above the gate, that you understand something more of Poland's history; her agony and her spiritual strength. You are closer to Russia. Belloc in 1938 wrote in the *Weekly Review* that the failure to control Danzig would ultimately mean the failure to control British predominance in Asia. In his article "Poland is the test," he wrote: "The determination to save Poland, which is a determination not only to defeat Prussia, but to oust the vile and murderous Communism of Moscow, is the moral condition of victory. If we waver we are lost."

Belloc had consistently fought the popular idea in England that the Treaty of Versailles was so unjust to the Germans that nobody could expect them to honour their signature. The more loudly the Germans protested against the treatment of them by the Allies, the more ready were we to listen, especially as it was to our advantage, politically and financially, to restore Germany as soon as possible to the place in Europe which she had lost: politically because a strong Germany, according to the old doctrine of the balance of power, would counteract a strong France: financially, because the bankers would (they hoped) get their interest on the money lent to Germany. To Belloc, the coming war was a war of religion, and for that reason he was irritated by all the silly clamour about "the cause of democracy." The coming war would not be fought by us in defence of a political system, but in defence of the religion and the civilization of Europe. And we should have not one enemy, but two enemies: Russia and Germany, each equally determined to destroy the moral code of Christendom, and to subjugate by armed force whatever should oppose them.

It is saddening to read now words which Belloc wrote after the attack on Poland:

> Unlike the Czechs, the Poles preferred to maintain their honour, and we may presume that this decision will guarantee their resurrection.

8

THE BREAKDOWN

WE TALK OF A "STUNNING BLOW." THE ADJECTIVE IS THE only one to use to describe the effect on Belloc of the defeat and collapse of France after so short a campaign. He was too bewildered and dazed to talk about it much. It was difficult to accept the fact that it had really happened.

Peter Belloc had a commission in the Royal Marines, and we saw each other occasionally while he was in training in southern England. Then he was moved, and I lost touch with him for a time. One day, when he was on leave, I lunched with him and his wife in London. It was a happy meeting, and he was in high spirits, as always, but my own thoughts were what the thoughts of a middle-aged man must be on such an occasion. He would be going into action soon. When we said goodbye, he gave me a little silver pencil, and he and his wife went away together. I never saw him again.

On the morning of April 2nd, 1941, I was in my office in

London. I was called to the telephone. The voice at the other end was indistinct, but after a moment or two it became clearer. It was my sister-in-law, who was living with us at the time, calling from Henfield, where a message had been sent to me. She said: "Peter Belloc is dead."

We agreed that she should ask Father Riley, the priest at West Grinstead, to take the news to King's Land. The rest of the day is a complete blank in my mind. I recall nothing, except that when I arrived home I was told that the priest had gone to King's Land and had broken the news to Belloc. Later, I heard the story of what had happened. Peter had been on a raid, and had returned home safely, unwounded, but had picked up some germ. He had gone into hospital in the north of England, and his condition was apparently not serious. But septicæmia developed, and very rapidly he became worse. By the grace of God, a priest in the hospital saw the signs of approaching death and gave him Absolution. His wife, summoned by telegram, arrived too late to see him alive.

My wife and I went over to King's Land on April 3rd and stayed a short time. Belloc said: "There is nothing to be said and nothing to be done." He came out of the house when we went away, and thanked us for our visit. His command over himself was complete, and this added to our own distress. It required little effort of the imagination to realize his desolation. Peter's body was brought to West Grinstead, and was buried in a grave next to his mother's. Belloc stood by himself, a little apart from the family, quite motionless. A few days later he came over to Henfield. He was exhausted, and complained of the cold. He said he would like to snatch a few minutes' sleep. So he sat in a chair, muffled in his cloak, with his feet stretched out to the fire, and was silent for a little while. I do not think he slept. After a time, he opened his eyes. Suddenly he said: "He was such a happy boy, wasn't he?

Such a happy disposition, always." I told him that Peter
had been my closest and dearest friend, and what that
friendship had meant to me, and he said quietly: "I know."
His daughter Eleanor Jebb told me later that it was at
this time that he began to lose his memory, and sometimes
confused Peter with Louis, the eldest son who had been
killed at the very end of the 1914–18 war.

A dinner was given to celebrate his seventy-first birthday, but he was exceedingly tired. He made a short reply
to Duff Cooper's speech in praise of his poetry, and then
left early in the evening, as he was anxious to catch his
train to Horsham. It was, I thought, a sad evening, and
there were no songs. He seemed to have grown much
older.

For the rest of that year he was very unhappy, and restless, not with his customary restlessness, but as though he
were perpetually bewildered and confused. I have a letter
from Marie Belloc Lowndes, written to me in October
1941. She says: "I am very unhappy about H. I think
Peter's death dealt him a mortal blow." But his daughter
Eleanor and her husband, who were looking after him at
King's Land, noticed a change after Christmas. His health
seemed to be better, and he was recovering from the
shock of Peter's death. Then on January 30th, 1942, he had
a slight stroke and fell at the Reform Club. He was put to
bed, but that night there was an air raid, and no word
arrived at King's Land until February 1st. He was brought
home, and Eleanor Jebb came over to Henfield to tell us
what had happened, and to talk over what should be done.
My wife rang up the Bon Secours nuns, and a Sister was
sent down to King's Land. The doctor said his heart was
affected. On February 2nd he developed pneumonia, and
on February 3rd he was anointed by the priest from West
Grinstead. That afternoon my wife and I went to King's

Land. Eleanor Jebb told us that he was conscious, but she did not think he could live through the night. When I went up to his bedroom he was lying on his back, breathing uneasily, but he greeted me cheerfully and when I asked how he was he said in a weak voice, "Oh, I'm all right," then, after a moment: "There was a fool called Coué—a Frenchman. He said: 'Every day in every way I get better and better.' Well, that's how it is with me." We talked for a while, and then the Sister brought him a glass of milk, which he refused vigorously. "Tell them," he said, "to take that filthy stuff away and bring me a glass of wine." I passed this on to the Sister, who did not like the idea at all. But my wife managed to convince her that a man who has been drinking wine all his life is none the better for having it suddenly cut off. So he had his glass of wine, and, listening to his talk, I could not believe that he was going to die, ill though he was.

His daughter sat up with him all that night, to give the Sister some sleep, and, although his heart was feeble, he slowly regained his strength—with wine and brandy and M and B as his medicines. He was in bed until the end of April, and when he finally got up and dressed and came downstairs, his mind was still jumbled and confused. By the autumn he was—not his old self—but amazingly recovered. He chafed very much against the impossibility of getting about, as, of course, he was much slower on his feet, and the war made it out of the question to travel at all. He came to London with us occasionally, and visited his friends in the country whenever he could, but his powers of concentration had gone, and he found it very difficult to dictate to Dorothy Collins, who had been Chesterton's secretary. But the gaiety was still there, and the good talk on every subject—except the war. He could not understand what had happened.

He used to ask me repeatedly: "Do you think the English will ever turn against the Germans? Will anything ever cure them of their admiration for the Boche?" The idea that any such admiration could remain seemed ridiculous to me, with the air raids, and everything else the Germans had done. You had only to listen to any conversation in a bar to hear what the English thought about the Germans. Belloc, of course, admitted that most Englishmen, for the moment, loathed the Germans. But his contention was that the educated classes, the moulders of public opinion, were not likely to lose that traditional love of Germany in which the universities were soaked during his Oxford days. I disagreed with him, but I was startled when some highly intelligent people with whom he and I were lunching during the war began to praise the Germans, and to imply that their gifts of organization and administration fitted them to rule Europe. Only Belloc's good manners restrained him. I was too angry to behave reasonably, and said what I knew we were both thinking. There were also people to whom the German claim that Germany was the bulwark against Russia and Marxism made a strong appeal. They must have been very happy to see, how soon after this second war, we adopted that idea, and could not do enough to get the Germans armed again. Then abominable and ridiculous war trials satisfied the hatred of Germany during the first war, but that, very quickly, she had been reinstated, because she was supposed to have had the famous "change of heart." I remembered Stresemann, "the good European," and the bilking of the French, for fear they might become too powerful. Belloc maintained to the end of his life that whatever we said about the Germans, the admiration would remain. Was he so wrong? The abominable and ridiculous war trials satisfied the hatred of the moment, and then, once more, Germany was to be re-armed, and the French were once more abused for their antagonism to the idea of a new German Army, and for refusing to do what we ourselves refused to do. We, of course, could not join the European Army, because of our commitments overseas—as though Indo-China was not a commitment overseas. Sometimes it was said that we could not commit ourselves too deeply in Europe, for fear of offending the countries of our Empire; and sometimes it was said that if we joined the European Army, it would draw us away from America. Both objections were worthless. What both our Empire and America wanted was a strong, united Europe. It was not France which had wrecked the plan of E.D.C., but England, as became apparent when England finally agreed to join.

Belloc had been accustomed all his life to meeting informed people and to hearing the questions of the day debated. His physical infirmity and the conditions of war kept him at home, and he was mystified. His brain, as the war went on, remained active, and as he began to regain his physical health, his vivacity returned, and he accepted the new conditions, but with an air of puzzlement. His movements had become very difficult, but he bore this handicap with great good humour, making a jest of his "immense age." He wrote no more, but read all the papers he could get hold of, and the books which had always been his favourites, such as Rabelais. In 1943 the Prime Minister asked him if he would accept a C.H. He begged to refuse the honour. He never cared at all for honours, and when, in 1934, the Pope made him a Knight of the Order of St. Gregory the Great, he neither paid the fee nor claimed the medal and ribbon. He said: "This will make me an official Catholic. What fools they'd all look, if I said in my next book that God doesn't exist." The button of the

Legion of Honour he wore only when he was travelling in France, because it eased things with officials.

*   *   *   *   *

We used to go into Horsham once a week or so for lunch towards the end of the war, in a hired car. He could never understand why the food was so scanty and so appallingly bad, but in the end we used to make a joke of the whole thing, wondering which delicacy we would select. Usually he would eat a plateful of soup and as much bread as he could get. One or other of us would go raiding all over the room, brazenly taking the bread from other tables. Sometimes we both raided at the same time, and people stared, as though to say, "Why don't they steal something worth stealing?" They would glance at the waitress, but she knew that nothing would keep us from our bread. Often, from old habit, Belloc put a hunk into the pocket of his cloak for future use.

He always wanted to go to London, but I used to dissuade him, as it tired him out, and exasperated him. It was better to sit at ease in Horsham, and I painted for him a picture of London which I hoped would keep him away from it. He also missed his travels abroad. The last time he had gone to France was early in 1940, when he had found his old regiment in the Maginot line, and had stood the officers champagne. We talked little of the war, and, without his appointments to keep or plans to make, he was less impatient than he had been. Also, he was sleeping better, no doubt because for the first time in his life he was resting, and not worried by work. But getting into and out of the car was an increasing difficulty, and he walked like a man far older than he was. He still sang when he felt inclined to, and had made a tune for Ronsard's *Quand Vous Serez Bien Vieille.* . . . Neither his speaking nor his singing voice had lost any of its power, and on many an occa-

sion time and place were forgotten as the manly chorus
rang out:

> Oh, I loved her to distraction,
> As I've often said before.
> She waddled like a duck, and she
> went pit-pat
> All over the kitchen floor.

He talked often of his old friend Maurice Baring, who
lay dying in Scotland; what impressed Belloc so much was
the strength and cheerfulness with which Baring bore his
sufferings. The last letter I had from Baring, a year before
his death, was dictated to his nurse. He said. "The night
before last I made up three ballades in my sleep. I remembered them when I woke up. The rhymes were all right,
but they made complete nonsense, and now I've forgotten
them altogether—except the rhymes. Do you ever see
Hilary?" Baring, of course, was bedridden, but Belloc's
other friends came to see him at King's Land whenever
they could. The change in him was a shock to those who
had not seen him for some time, but he was still such good
company that it was he who cheered up the dispirited. It
was remarkable that a man who had been so impatient
was able to adapt himself so philosophically to a life without occupation. Of course he grumbled. But he had always grumbled—in his own humorous fashion, as though
he were laughing at himself for allowing things to irritate
him. He even accustomed himself to the perpetual noise
in the sky. One day while we were having a meal at Henfield there was a raid. A bomb was dropped in a field close
to our house, and one of the planes swooped, and machine-
gunned the little place. Belloc took no notice, and made
no remark. But on another occasion he was very badly
shaken when a plane crashed in the field where the tennis
court at King's Land used to be, not many yards from the

house. The dead pilot was brought into King's Land. There was a landing ground only a few miles away from Shipley, and there was no more of the quiet which he had been used to there.

In 1945 took place the clothing ceremony of my god-child Marianne Jebb, who was to become a Canoness of St. Augustine at the Priory in Haywards Heath. Belloc, who had been devoted to her, was very sad at losing her. Her three brothers were on the altar at the Mass, and Stella Belloc and her children, and Douglas Woodruff, were there. It was interesting to remember that Elodie Hogan, Belloc's future wife, had gone into a convent for a time, but had discovered that she had no vocation, that Eleanor, her daughter, had had the same experience, and that now, in the third generation, the experiment was being repeated—but this time there was a vocation. Belloc was deeply moved, as he always was by two things: the innocence of children, and holiness. He often said to me that holiness is unmistakable, and that he always felt it strongly when he was in the presence of Father Vincent McNabb. He talked of his granddaughter a great deal afterwards, and missed her very much at King's Land. His memory was becoming worse, and he was quite aware of it. He used to ask me, "How old am I?", and when I told him, he would say, "Good God! What an age to be!" He talked sometimes about his work, and always said that he wanted his verse to endure, but that he thought such a small output was against him. My own opinion was that his versatility was against him, as people today cannot believe that a writer can do a number of things really well. They like specialization. A novelist is a novelist, a poet is a poet, and so on. To someone who had once asked him why he wrote so much, he had answered: "Because my children are howling for pearls and caviar."

He talked no more about money. When he was in his

full health and strength he had always had to think of money. He had never been secure, and it was obvious that his books would not bring in the regular income to which more popular writers can look forward for the comfort of their declining years. More money would have enabled him to make things easier for those who were, to varying extents, dependent upon him. His own tastes were simple. He travelled cheaply, and did not mind living rough. Money, also, would have given him a chance of working less hard, and he said to me once that he wanted to stop writing at seventy, and rest. But I think he would never have stopped. He would have written more slowly, and would have given us his Memoirs, which were not to be published until after his death. He did make an attempt to start them some years after the second war, and tried to dictate to Dorothy Collins, but it was no good. He could not concentrate, and the task was abandoned. I often met people who seemed to be astounded that he was not a rich man, because his name was so well known to them; but though he had entertained so many with his writing, he had told unpleasant truths. He was writing against his time, against the beliefs of the age in which he lived, and he kept faith with himself. "In the matter of personal honour," he said to me, "we all ought to behave as though we were millionaires." In the words of Yeats, he

> never made a poorer song,
> that he might have a heavier purse.

In 1946 my wife and I went to live in Ireland. A day or two before we left England we drove Belloc over to Itchenor, to say goodbye to Elsie Allison, now Elsie Quick, and her husband. We had a very lively lunch, and then came back to King's Land. We drove through Slindon, and Belloc told us stories of his boyhood there, and pointed out the house of the man who had taught him to sail. Under

Duncton Hill we sang in chorus the song about Pelagius, or, to give it its full and noble title, The Song of the Pelagian Heresy for the Strengthening of Men's Backs and the Very Robust Outthrusting of Doubtful Doctrine and the Uncertain Intellectual. We stopped the car, and the song rolled out across the peaceful countryside, semi-chorus, full chorus and all. Belloc was then in his seventy-seventh year, but his voice had certainly lost none of its power. After the song was over, Echo having plugged her ears, we started off again and came very merrily to King's Land. It was a day of happiness, but a sad occasion. Belloc was sorry to see us go as, being such near neighbours, it was easier for us to drop in on him than for his other friends. He talked of coming to stay with us in Ireland. As for me, I could not pretend to myself that he would ever make a complete recovery, and there was no companionship I cared for as much as his.

On our way to Liverpool we broke the journey at South Moreton in Berkshire, where Stella Belloc lived, and the three children clamoured for news of their grandfather, to whom they were all devoted. They were never tired of hearing stories of him and of their father, and the Belloc songs were sung in their house as they had been at Rodmell, and wherever the friends of the family met.

The next year we came to England for a few days, and I saw a change in Belloc. Physically, he seemed well, and when I asked him how he was, he said: "Very cheerful." But the change was in his eyes. The life seemed to have gone out of them. They were sad and, in some curious way, perplexed. He walked very slowly and sat down and got up with greater difficulty than before, and he was more silent than I had ever known him. We sat in his study, and he smoked his pipe, and appeared to be trying to get clear in his mind where I had come from. He complained of his memory, and said: "I shall forget my own name next." After a while, however, he began to talk in the old way, but with less verve. His manner was gentler. There was no grumbling, not even about his enforced inactivity. I think he had perhaps seen the approach of death, and, as he told me once, "A man is a fool who says he is not frightened of death. If he could know what the moment of death is really like, the thought would be unbearable." He had braced himself to meet what was to come, and what was revealed in his character was fortitude. Of fortitude he once wrote that it is "the virtue of the menaced, of the beleaguered. . . . It is the converse to and the opposite of aggressive flamboyant courage, yet it is the greater of the two though often it lacks action. Fortitude wears armour and holds a sword. It stands ready rather than thrusts forward. It demands no supplement; it is nourished not from without but from within. It is replenished of its own substance. . . . Sometimes fortitude will earn fame, but not often. Always, however, it will earn reward." His life had been full of aggressive courage. His last years showed his fortitude. "Fortitude," he wrote, "is primarily Endurance: that character which we need the most in the dark business of life. But if fortitude be endurance, it is also creative endurance, and at the same time it involves some memory of better times and some expectation of their return. It involves, therefore, fidelity and hope; and, without these two, fortitude would be of little use: but, above all, fortitude is endurance."[1]

That sad and perplexed look in his eyes was, I have no doubt, no more than a manifestation of his clouded mind, but every time I met him after that I was more and more struck by his quiet courage. He said repeatedly, "How short is human life! How quickly it passes! Here am I with one foot in the grave," and, pushing out his foot, "This one!" The new gentleness of his manner emphasized his

[1] "On Fortitude." (*The Silence of the Sea*. Sheed & Ward: 1940.)

unfailing courtesy. Then, suddenly, would come a flash of
his old self, and a loud song, or a barrack-room jest.

Enforced idleness and the inability to be constantly
mixing with people were difficult for him to bear with
patience, and everything possible was done by his daughter and his son-in-law to encourage his friends to visit him.
He was never happier than when surrounded by his
grandchildren, but when there were many people at
King's Land, he appeared confused, and kept rather in the
background, though he liked the coming and going, and
the noise of talk.

On one of our short visits to England we went with him
to lunch with James and Pauline Gunn in London. Gunn
had just started another portrait of him. Belloc kept us all
happy throughout the meal, and later we drove him to
Victoria to get the train back to Horsham. He was very
tired and seemed overwhelmed by the noise and bustle of
the station. He looked round him uncertainly, and stopped
once or twice. We saw him into the train, and the guard,
who knew him well, made him comfortable. Though he
was to be met at Horsham, we were alarmed at his helplessness, and at his obvious unfitness for journeys. I could
not get used to that air of bewilderment.

*   *   *   *   *

We came to England for a short stay every year, and we
noticed very little change in Belloc. His unusually strong
constitution seemed, in fact, to have arrested his decline.
He led a quiet and regular life at King's Land, and still
went occasionally to stay with friends and there were always people to visit him at home. He had become a patri-
archal figure, with a long grey beard and thick whiskers
and moustache. He walked with the aid of his blackthorn
stick, a few steps at a time, and he would look startled for
a moment when he saw anyone whom he did not know

well. Then he would shake hands, with that old-fashioned bow. He was less inclined now to start a conversation himself, but any question addressed to him would set his mind in motion, and his talk was always interesting, even now, especially when he spoke of time long past. And he was ready to sing on the slightest provocation in the light voice which had lost none of its clarity.

In the summer of 1949 Peter Belloc's eldest daughter, Gabrielle Elodie, was married in London to Douglas Blyth, and the next year I gave away his second daughter, my godchild Barbara. It was something of a business for Belloc to undertake any journey now, but at the first of these weddings he was surrounded by friends, and kept everybody entertained. While I was making a speech, I could hear his voice across the room, and it was difficult, without looking at him, to realize how very old he had become. Yet there seemed to be something indestructible about him, and we all agreed that he would probably live for many more years. But when Zita Mary, the third Belloc girl, and my wife's godchild, was married, he could not manage the journey from his home.

We came back to England in the autumn of 1949. In July 1950, Belloc celebrated his eightieth birthday, and the Press suddenly discovered that there was a great man to be honoured. There were tributes from all sides, but he had had to wait a long time for them, and was now beyond caring very much. Douglas Woodruff, Robert Speaight and I had lunch with him at King's Land, and other friends came in groups to celebrate his birthday. On every occasion on which I saw him after that I was more and more impressed by his spirit; by his fortitude. He always said, when I asked him how he was: "I'm very cheerful." But he always expressed his astonishment at the "shortness of human life." We used to sit and talk in his study, and his mind was more and more in the past. He told me

once that he had thought of staying in the French Army,
when his service was completed, but that his family was
against it. His battery was going East, and it is interesting
to speculate on what might have happened. He would
probably have served under Joffre or Gallieni, and might
have been a French General in the 1914–18 war. He was a
man who had enjoyed to the full his experiences as a soldier; the companionship, the full use of the body, the
servitude et grandeur militaires, the grousing that ended
in song, the wide landscape, the deep sleep of youth in
barns. Soldiering was in his blood, and one of Peter Belloc's proudest possessions was the watch carried by
Armand   Swanton,   his   French   great-grandmother's
brother, in the Moscow campaign.

On another occasion Belloc said: "I sometimes wish I'd
remained in California." He talked much of its beauty,
and it was, of course, to California he had come, after
walking across America, to claim the girl he had fallen in
love with at first sight in a house in Westminster—the
Irish-American Elodie Hogan, who lived at Napa. When
he wondered whether some other kind of life would not
have been happier than the toil of incessant writing, he
was thinking of his youth, with a wife and a young family,
and of the refusal to grant him an Oxford Fellowship.
That refusal he could never forget. It would have given
him a background, a position. In these last years he was
still talking of the dons as he had talked of them all
through his life—and of the "professional politicians." I
told him one day about some argument or other in the
House, and he said: "Is that bloody nonsense still going
on?" I said that indeed it was. "Very well," he said, and
paused. Then, in the solemn and measured tone of a man
who is entrusting an important message to a friend: "Tell
them from me to go to Hell!"

He thought a good deal about his verse, and was always

wondering whether it would survive. "I should very much like it to." He was annoyed that the lines:

> There's nothing worth the wear of winning
> But laughter and the love of friends

were quoted so often. He said they were bad verse, and were only remembered because of the alliteration. He also disliked the well-known poem about Balliol. Of the sonnet "O my companion, O my sister, sleep," he told me that Arnold Bennett had said that it didn't mean anything. As we sat together, I noticed longer silences than usual. He would stare into the fire or out of the window, and then, as though to shake off some unwelcome thought, he would break into song—sometimes a song I had never heard before, and when I asked what it was, he would say: "I don't know. Something I heard when I was young. I don't know where."

He talked about La Celle-St-Cloud, and his French uncles and aunts and cousins, and his mother's dislike of the British Empire. "I hate the name," she used to say, "and I hate the thing." Sometimes he spoke of going abroad again, but I think he knew that his travels were over. But whenever he referred to his infirmity, he made a joke of it, so that there was no question of sympathizing with him. It took him some time to realize that certain of his friends were dead, but Maurice Baring's lingering death had made a great impression on him, and he had said many years before in a letter to my wife, on the death of her father after long years of suffering:

> It is the supreme achievement of a Catholic so to die: and the great legacy he can leave to mankind. It is a very heavy burden to those who remain, this end of a long human tie of earth; and of the closest. But it is tolerable to those inside the Church.

"This morning," he said to me one day, "I found a letter from Peter. I can't tell you how it moved me."

Sometimes I arrived in time to sit with him while he had his breakfast. He used to come down about eleven o'clock. "I spend more and more time in bed," he said on one such occasion. "I go to bed earlier and get up later. Cut off at both ends as the *cul-de-jatte* said when they guillotined him." A violent fit of coughing seized him, completely exhausting him. "I'm so sorry," he said. "It's so distressing for you." After breakfast we would go into the study, and he would sit in an old armchair, and light and re-light a pipe which was always going out. If there were people in the drawing-room after lunch, he joined them, but sat apart, and did not talk much. He seemed to be bewildered by company, but when it was a question of singing, he became much more lively. When anyone left, he always came out to the little space in front of the house to see him or her off, and stood waving until the car turned the corner into the lane.

One St. Stephen's Day there was a great gathering at King's Land, with the children and grandchildren and a number of friends. The noise was so continuous that I thought Belloc would be bemused by it, but he thoroughly enjoyed it. He sang his own songs and many others. In the matter of his own songs, I have said that he always insisted on having them sung as they were composed. There was only one way of singing the last line of "You Wear the Morning like Your Dress." This is what we always called it, but its title is: "Song Inviting the Influence of a Young Lady upon the Opening Year." Again, there is only the one way of singing the last line of "The Winged Horse." And nobody could manage "Tarantella" or "The Chaunty of the *Nona*" to Belloc's complete satisfaction. As for "Strephon's Song," instead of singing very gently, "To implore for that delicate, delicate flower" he would sometimes bellow: "To go off like a hound for that delicate flower." While the songs were at their height the fourth generation came into the room; Barbara Eustace's baby girl. Her mother carried her in, and brought her to her great-grandfather, who was singing lustily at the head of the table. The huge blast of noise swept over her little head, and thus was she, who was quite unmoved, introduced to the noble tradition.

❋   ❋   ❋   ❋   ❋

Looking back on the end of Belloc's life, and then thinking of him as he was at the height of his powers, I am struck by the way in which a trait of his character which surprised even his intimate friends was revealed clearly. It would not have been surprising if a man renowned for his impatience had become still more impatient, when he found himself incapacitated. The reverse happened. And it was not that he did not know what had befallen him. He knew that his memory was impaired, and said so. He was himself growing feebler in body, and made a jest of it. One was tempted sometimes to find his patience distressing, and to wish for an outburst of complaint. His gentleness seemed unnatural, until one realized that it was edifying; that it was courage.

Sometimes sitting in his study and musing on the past, he recaptured for a moment old regrets and discouragements, but they no longer had power to wound him. They saddened him, but he would not allow the mood to command him, and exactly as he had always done, he would rout such thoughts with a song or a story. It was that courage which I remember best.

The only thing which neither age nor illness had changed was his voice. When talking, he had not, of course, the same emphatic manner. But the tone of his voice was the same. If you looked away from him, and

listened, it was difficult to believe that in other respects
he was so changed. I think he made enormous efforts to
dispel the clouds over his memory, for often, after a period
of silence, he would say: "Let me see now. Where is it
you've come from today? I can't understand what is going
on. I no longer remember anything." Then, a subject of
conversation once started, he would cease to worry, and
would talk of his boyhood at La Celle, of his Aunt Louise,
of the little school of artists which formed round his
grandfather Hilaire Belloc, of Colonel Swanton, who was
always called M. le Colonel in his family, and of his
mother's friendship with the great Victorian writers; and
as though it all seemed very near in time, he always ended
by saying: "I am appalled by the shortness of human life."

He did not seem to me to be growing any feebler, and
I thought that he might live another ten years. He walked
with greater difficulty, and no longer went more than a
few steps from the house, but his memory did not appear
to be getting worse. But his daughter told me that the
winter of 1952–3 had been a hard struggle for him. She, of
course, could judge better than an occasional visitor.
When I saw him in that winter, he said no word about his
health, but, as always, remarked: "How quickly life
passes." We talked in his study, and he said, as though he
had only just come to King's Land: "All my life I've been
accustomed to a landscape, a horizon. Here one is shut in."
As we drank our sherry he said: "There will be wine in
Heaven." He hummed a song, lit and re-lit his pipe, and
the afternoon passed pleasantly away in reminiscences
and anecdotes. When I rose to go, he got out of his chair
with difficulty, and I stretched out my hand to help him,
but he put it aside. He never liked being assisted. He came
very slowly from the study and through the drawing-
room, and waved as I set out.

Looking back, I saw him standing before the house, a

lonely figure, the great shoulders shrunken with age and sickness, the eyes, once so animated, now forlorn. He remained, leaning on his blackthorn,[1] until I turned the corner of the house.

> I said to Heart: "How goes it?" Heart replied: "Right as a ribstone pippin." But it lied.

❋　　❋　　❋　　❋　　❋

On the eve of his twelfth birthday, Mrs. Belloc Lowndes tells us, his "Tante Jenny," Mme Bibron, had written to the boy Hilaire:

> Try to work steadfastly and constantly, my dear Hilaire, for thus alone is happiness to be found. In work, also, can be found that tranquillity of soul which nothing can destroy.

He had worked steadfastly and constantly, but had not found happiness. At the end, when his work was done, I think he had found tranquillity of soul.

[1] This blackthorn was given to him on June 19th 1923, at the Mansion House in Dublin, by Tim Healy. Among those who heard his speech, and watched the presentation, was my future wife. It is now in our house.

9

HIS DEATH

Sunday, july 12th, 1953, was a cold, wet day at Shipley. Belloc remained late in bed, and had his break-fast—his usual coffee and bread and butter—in his room. A fire was lit for him in his study, and he dressed and came down about 11.30. His daughter noticed that he seemed unwell and ill at ease. He was restless, and went to and fro between his study and the drawing-room, where he talked to two young people who were in the house, Rosemary Sheed, and a friend of Julian Jebb. Eventually he settled down in the study, and about 12.45 his daughter brought him some sherry, and saw to the fire. After that he wandered about again. His daughter heard him go back to the study. She and Rosemary Sheed were in the kitchen preparing lunch, and shortly after one o'clock there was a smell of something burning. Eleanor Jebb ran from the kitchen, through the dining-room, where her father's coat was lying on the table, and into the study. There was smoke in the room. Belloc lay on the floor, near the fireplace, and a piece of coal which had fallen from the grate, and which he had evidently tried to replace, was lying on the carpet. His shirt and vest were smouldering, and he said: "My darling, I need help." Julian Jebb was called, and they threw a rug round him and got him into his armchair. He drank some sherry, and, as Eleanor Jebb said: "For the first time in my life I saw his hand shake." The burns, of themselves, were not very bad, but the shock had been too much for him. The village nurse was soon at the house, and did what could be done. The doctor arrived soon after, and Belloc, to quote his daughter again, "Had a grand slanging match with him." A bed was put up in the study, and a room was engaged at a Catholic nursing home in Guildford. At four o'clock the ambulance drew up. Belloc did not appear to be in pain, but his face was very white. He said he was all right, and that he could not understand what the fuss was about. But he made no complaint, and accepted the whole thing quietly and patiently.

He was anointed on the Monday evening, and was then given an anæsthetic. During the Tuesday he had alternating periods of consciousness and unconsciousness, and on Wednesday morning, July 15th, he seemed to be a little better. Lady Phipps was with him for a while. In the evening Philip Jebb, his eldest grandson, gave him a glass of red wine. But the improvement was only temporary, and on the morning of the 16th, Thursday, Stella Belloc and her sister Zita Anderson drove me over to Guildford. We stopped at Horsham, to take with us Edith, the faithful maid who had been with the family since 1906, the year King's Land became their home. When we arrived at the nursing home, Elizabeth Belloc came out to us and said that he was unconscious and was not expected to live through the day. It seemed unbelievable to me, and I half expected some astonishing recovery. When I saw him, I knew that there was no hope. He was lying slightly raised in the bed, with his eyes closed, and was breathing loudly and rapidly, like a runner who is out of breath. His face was very pale. As we watched him, there would come a sudden check in the breathing, and complete silence. Then the same hurried rhythm would recommence. Elizabeth Belloc gave out the Rosary, and then we remained watching round the bed. Even then, I could not help thinking that he would become conscious, and open his eyes, and ask what the fuss was about. We went out for something to eat, and when we came back there was no change. But very soon, the breathing became quieter. It was still hurried, but no longer loud. The priest said the prayers for the dying.

Reginald Jebb and Eleanor and I went to Benediction in the chapel above the room, and when the nuns sang:

> *Qui vitam sine termino*
> *Nobis donet in patria*

I recalled how he once wrote that he believed those words not only with all the strength of his emotion but with all the power of his intellect. Always he had returned, in his writing and his talk, to that theme of a coming out of exile into our native land.

When we returned to the death-bed, there still seemed to be no change, but the nurse said that there was now hardly any pulse. The priest came back, and as we prayed in silence the breathing of the dying man grew fainter, until it was little more than a whisper of sound in the room. A thrush was singing loudly outside the window. The nurse made a movement, looked up, and nodded. Even as we watched, the lips, which had been so pale, became paler still, and we knew that he was dead.

❋   ❋   ❋   ❋   ❋

He was buried at West Grinstead, where lie his wife and his son Peter, and Pauline Gunn, in the shadow of the tall cross of the war memorial which fronts the road along which he used to come to Mass. Among the names on the memorial is that of Louis Belloc, the eldest son, whose body was never found. At the base of the cross are carved those words which sum up all the hope of the living: *O Crux Ave Spes Unica.*

❀   ❀   ❀   ❀   ❀

One thing in this world is different from all other. It has a personality and a force. It is recognized, and (when recognized) most violently loved or hated. It is the Catholic Church. Within that household the human spirit has roof and hearth. Outside it, is the Night.

> *In hac urbe lux sollennis,*
> *Ver æternum, pax perennis,*
> *et æterna gaudia.*